Easy
Wedding Planner

Easy
Wedding
Planner

JENNY HOPKIN

GUILD OF MASTER CRAFTSMAN PUBLICATIONS

First published 2004 by
Guild of Master Craftsman Publications Ltd,
166 High Street, Lewes,
East Sussex, BN7 1XN

Cover photography by Chris Skarbon, except left and right back cover inserts,
by Anthony Bailey
Inside photography by Anthony Bailey, except: pages 9, 12, 14, 25, 56, 57, 59, 60, 74,
86, 87, 88, 90, 93, 112, 113, 116, 120, 121, 129, 132, 133, 135 all © copyright Corbis;
and pages 13, 15, 54 by Tim Hull
With thanks to Sheila Marshall Fashions, Lewes, for the loan of background fabrics

ISBN 1 86108 328 9

Publisher: Paul Richardson
Art Director: Ian Smith
Production Manager: Stuart Poole
Managing Editor: Gerrie Purcell
Commissioning Editor: April McCroskie
Editor: Clare Miller
Designer: Maggie Aldred

Colour origination by Icon Reproduction, UK

Printed and bound by Sino Publishing House, Hong Kong, China

Dedication

To Liz, Tim and Elaine for their help
with *our* wedding, to our parents for allowing us
to have the wedding we wanted and, most of all,
to Neil – if he'd not been willing to marry me,
this book would never have come into being!

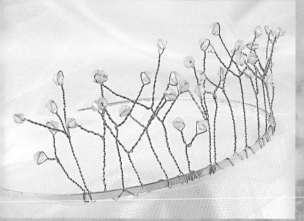

Contents

Introduction

The cost of getting married is growing. Weddings are big business and unfortunately some companies hike up their prices to make even more money out of your big day. Many couples long to get married, but put it off because they think that they can't afford to. However, you don't have to spend that much if you can't or don't want to. You can get married for very little and still have a wonderful day. My own wedding cost the same in total as the average price of a wedding dress, including a fortnight's honeymoon in idyllic Costa Rica and the whole thing was far from being average!

Many specialist wedding companies might offer goods and services that are out of your budget, but the inspiration that they offer is free. A recurrent theme throughout this book is that you can copy or adapt designs and ideas to suit your day and your wallet. Get samples of invitations and place cards and use them to inspire your own designs. Look at photographers' websites and see what style of photos you like – then ask your photographer to take similar photos at your wedding. See if you can persuade Auntie Betty to muster all her baking skills and recreate that designer chocolate wedding cake!

This book is not about wedding etiquette. There are plenty of books that tell you who should stand where in your receiving line and what a best man's duties are.

This book is intended to inspire you to have a go at tackling some areas of your wedding yourself – to be a 'do-it-yourself' bride. You might want to make your own invitations, arrange your own flowers or decorate your own cake. In addition to saving money, you'll probably have fun and gain a lot of satisfaction from doing so, as well as ensuring that your wedding is unique and individual.

This book won't turn you into an expert cake decorator, florist or jeweller, but it will give you ideas and inspiration, plus the basic skills you need, to tackle making your own cake, bouquet and even tiara. If you don't fancy making your own things, there are also ideas on how to cheat; with the right decoration, none of your guests will ever guess that your beautiful cake came from the local supermarket!

Please note These days, people get married in a diverse range of locations. For the sake of simplicity, I have used the word 'church' as a generic term throughout this book to refer to the place where the ceremony takes place. Likewise, I've used the word 'venue' to refer to the place where the reception takes place. Of course, you can get married in a wide variety of places and you might even choose to have your ceremony and reception in the same place. Wherever you are getting married, you should find it easy to adapt the ideas in this book to suit your big day.

CHAPTER 1

Why Plan Your Own Wedding?

Some important things to consider before becoming a do-it-yourself bride.

The most obvious reason to have a do-it-yourself (DIY) wedding is cost. Perhaps you don't have the kind of money that it takes to pay for the average wedding, or perhaps you would simply rather spend it elsewhere. Organizing and making elements of your wedding can undoubtedly save you money, but there are other good reasons for doing so.

We've all heard of weddings where the caterers had allowed only one slice of ham and a chicken drumstick per person and where the only thing in limitless supply was lettuce. Or where the profiteroles and cheesecake disappeared leaving only a piece of fruit, some cheese and a cream cracker for latecomers to the dessert table. At a DIY wedding, you are in control. With the catering, it is up to you what is served and how much is provided. You also have the security of knowing, as you walk up the aisle, that everything is going to be just as you want it, because you aren't dependent on any outside suppliers, who are, after all, only there to make money. There is also the satisfaction of knowing that your wedding is unique, as well as the benefit of the new skills you'll acquire and the sense of camaraderie as your friends and family help you to make your day special.

However, there are downsides to a DIY wedding. Think carefully before making the decision to undertake one, as they take a lot of time and preparation and are not for everyone. You might spend every evening for months making sugar-paste roses, cake, invitations, table decorations – the list is endless. Organizing a wedding can be stressful for any bride, and you will have far more work as a DIY bride.

Always bear in mind that it's your special day and know when to draw the line – you need to do whatever makes you feel special. If you want that gorgeous designer dress, then buy it! Don't take too much on – do the things you'd like to do and leave the rest to the professionals.

Bear in mind that it's your special day. Don't take too much on and do whatever you need to feel special

My story

I married Neil in 1999. We didn't initially plan to have a DIY wedding but ended up doing practically everything ourselves. It turned out to be one of the most positive experiences of my life.

One of the first things you think about when you've just got engaged and have started to plan your big day is the invitations, and it was with the invitations that my DIY experience began. We looked on the internet and on the high street and simply couldn't find anything we particularly liked. I had always fancied trying to make hand-made greetings cards so I had a go at a couple of designs and we chose the one we liked best. We then got on with the long and laborious business of making a hundred cards, printing the inserts on our computer and sending them off. Inevitably, once we had made all the invitations, we had to make a start on the orders of service and thank you cards. We made these out of the same hand-made papers and miniature roses as our invitations and bought everything from local craft shops.

Inspired by the invitations, we decided to have a go at the cake. I'd never got beyond Victoria sponge before, but I got really into it, reading sugarcraft magazines and visiting specialist shops. It was a three-tiered, rich fruit cake covered in sugar roses and ivy leaves, which took hours and hours to make. I did

one rose every evening after work for what seemed like months. But it was very satisfying.

I didn't make my own dress, but I did make my veil, spending every lunchtime sewing beads and sequins onto it – I did it at work so that it would be a surprise for Neil. The office floor ended up sparkling with all the decoration that had been dropped in the process! My friend Elaine also helped me make the bridesmaid's dress for my sister Liz.

I'm no expert at make-up, so I'd decided that this was a job for the professionals. I went for a free

I didn't initially plan to have a 'DIY' wedding but it turned out to be one of the most positive experiences of my life

I made my own veil whilst at work in order to keep it a secret!

impressed our guests the most. We never intended to cater for the wedding ourselves, but we couldn't find a caterer we liked and most of them seemed overpriced. We wanted an informal buffet with all our favourite foods in plentiful supply and DIY seemed the best way to ensure that we got this on a reasonable budget. In the end, we had about 90 guests – the most I'd ever catered for before was a dinner party for six!

I have to admit that we cheated and bought lots of ready-made things from a supermarket that offers a special order catering service. We bought a selection of luxurious things like pork pies topped with cranberries, lovely patés and salmon hors d'oeuvres and Elaine cooked and dressed three whole salmon for us.

I was up at five in the morning on the day of the wedding to make huge vegetarian quiches and chocolate eclairs. It was pandemonium as we lived in a small studio flat and my parents, my sister and I were all crammed into the tiny kitchen together. Meanwhile Neil was picking up our order from the supermarket and another friend Sarah helped him arrange everything artistically on the buffet table at the church hall.

It was a lot of work, but well worth it when several of the guests said it was the best wedding food they'd ever tasted. A couple of

make-over in a large department store, bought everything they recommended and took careful notes about how to apply it. On the day I only had five minutes to do my make-up because I was still up to my eyes in baking chocolate eclairs!

Although I'd bought jewellery, including a tiara, by the week of the wedding I'd decided that I wanted to have a go at that too! With just days to go, I bought beads, tiara bases and silver wire and spent hours threading beads onto wire to make tiaras, necklaces and earrings.

But of all the things we did ourselves, I suppose the catering was the most daunting task. It was also the aspect of our wedding that

unexpected guests showed up but there was plenty of food so it was no problem to squeeze them in. Some people even went home with food parcels – a far cry from the horror stories I'd heard about weddings where the caterers had counted everything down to the last sausage on a stick.

Our friend Tim nobly agreed to take the photos. Another friend did the video and we hired a white London taxi to take me to the church. Neil is an ordained vicar so in theory he could even have done the ceremony himself!

Doing so much of the wedding ourselves was the best thing we've ever done. We got so many compliments on the day and really felt we had achieved something. It was reassuring knowing exactly what to expect, with no possibility of a nasty surprise from the caterers or any other suppliers. There was a huge sense of camaraderie: I was amazed at how supportive and kind our friends were – some even stayed on to help with the washing up after the reception.

Undeniably, it helped our budget too! Catering for 90 guests cost far less than if we'd hired caterers, and we could have easily spent half that and still fed everybody. The entire cost of the wedding, including our honeymoon, came in at far less than the average wedding.

There were evenings when I was tired and didn't want to face making yet another sugar rose. But the only really negative feeling was the sense of anticlimax when it was all over.

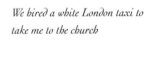

We hired a white London taxi to take me to the church

CHAPTER 2

Planning Your Budget

However large or small your budget, it's important to decide how to allocate it as soon as you can.

*P*robably your main motivation for going DIY is financial, so it's important to set a budget and stick to it. But beware! Producing elements of your own wedding is not always cheaper. Learning a new skill and putting it into practice can be costly.

For example, just to make my cake, I had to buy three large cake tins, two books, pillars, several tools for making sugar roses and three large storage containers. That was before I bought any ingredients. I have used most of these things since, but if you don't think you will it might be sensible to think about buying your cake. With everything you are thinking of making, work out what you'll need and cost it out, before going ahead.

Consider the half-way option too. Still on the subject of cakes, you can buy ready-made, ready-iced cakes in supermarkets in a variety of sizes that you can then place on tiers or a cake-stand and decorate. This might be the cheapest option on a budget. In several chapters in this book, there are suggestions for other half-way options.

There are some areas you might want to splash out on.

Consider your priorities:

♥ if looking good on your big day is top of the list, spend more on your dress, your hair and your make-up

♥ rings are something you'll wear forever, so you might regret economizing on them

♥ if you don't get the photos you want of your big day, you will regret it, so think carefully before handing that responsibility over to an amateur.

When you've worked out what
you have to spend and where your
priorities lie, draw up an itemized
budget. You can use the table on the
following pages as a guide. It is helpful
to find out the current average cost of
each item so you can be realistic about
how much you hope to spend, then
work out your own target budget.
Fill in the 'Actual cost' column as you
go so that you can work out where you
have spent over and under your
target budget and modify further
spending accordingly. The final
'How?' column provides ideas on
how to make savings.

*You can buy ready-made iced
cakes from most supermarkets*

ITEM

	Average cost	My budget	Actual cost
Rings			
Bride's outfit: *Dress*			
Veil and head-dress			
Shoes			
Hair and make-up			
Bouquet			
Going-away outfit			
Bridesmaids' outfits			
Groom and attendants' outfits			
Ceremony: *Church*			
Music			
Reception: *Venue*			
Venue decoration			
Entertainment			
Catering: *Food*			
Drink			
Cake			
Photographs/video			
Transport			
Honeymoon			
First-night hotel			
Stationery			
Insurance			
Contingency			
GRAND TOTAL			

How to make savings

Decide carefully whether you want to economize here, as you're going to wear your rings forever

Buy a pale-coloured evening dress from a department store

Make your 'something borrowed' a veil and head-dress from a friend or relative

Look for bargains in the end-of-season sales or buy a pair second-hand

Ask a talented girlfriend to help you with these!

Grow your own flowers to make a hand-tied bouquet and arrangements for your venue

Leave the reception venue in your wedding dress and change en route – that way you won't need a going-away outfit!

Ask your bridesmaids to wear a favourite outfit

Wear favourite suits rather than buying or hiring them specially

You may well have a favourite church in mind, but if not there are a huge range of approved premises of which you can research the prices

You won't need music in a registry office

Have the reception at home, perhaps in your garden if it's big enough

Keep it simple – a few carefully arranged fresh flowers from the garden can be very effective

Using a CD-rewriter, make compilation CDs of your favourite tracks

Get everyone to bring a dish - ensure everyone knows what to make so you don't just get desserts!

Ask your guests to bring a bottle

Buy from a supermarket and decorate or ask a friend to make it as your wedding present

Ask your friends to take your photos and ask one person to be in charge of videoing the wedding

Ask a friend with a special or unusual car to be your chauffeur as their wedding present to you

Borrow a cottage, a caravan or even a tent or ask for holiday vouchers as your wedding gifts

Look for cheap last-minute deals online

Design invitations on your PC. Email as many as possible to save on printing and postage

You could choose to risk having no insurance, though I would not advise this personally

CHAPTER 3

The Schedule

Draw up a schedule and plan your wedding with the precision of a military operation! It will save you time in the long run.

*I*f you haven't yet set the date for your wedding, that is probably the best place to start. There are lots of things to take into consideration regarding when you would like to get married. If you want to get married in a particular place or hold your reception at a specific venue, you might find that availability dictates your wedding date for you. There could be family reasons to consider, or you may want to choose a date that is special such as the anniversary of the date you first met.

If you know already where you would like to go on your honeymoon, that might be a deciding factor in setting the date too. When is the best time of year to go to your chosen destination? You don't want to end up visiting in the rainy season. If budget is a consideration, is there a cheaper time of year to go?

Consider arranging your wedding for a weekday or out-of-season. You could find that you receive discounts on many wedding goods and services. Try to avoid the most popular dates of the year.

Once you've set a date, you'll need to draw up a schedule for all the jobs that will need doing before and on the big day itself. But before you do that, you'll need to decide how much of your wedding you can do yourself. It may help to ask yourself some simple questions:

♥ Which parts of the wedding would you enjoy doing yourself? If you don't like sewing, it's not a good idea to attempt making the dress!

♥ When is the wedding? If it's still a year away, you can timetable things to do over that year, but be realistic about what can be achieved if you have less time than that.

♥ How much free time do you have? If you work long hours, don't undertake too much. If you find you are tired in the evenings, take into account that you may not always get a lot done.

♥ How much help can you realistically expect to get from family and friends?

Think about your circle of friends and family. If someone has a particular skill such as cake decorating they might be willing to donate their services instead of giving you a

Remember some things can be organized well in advance; your dress and your stationery, for example, could be made months ahead of the big day. If you're having a fruit cake, it will actually improve with age, so if you're making that yourself, start it as soon as you can. Other things, however, need to be done the day before, or even on the day itself. Unless you have lots of helpers, it might be wiser not to undertake both the catering and the flowers yourself.

wedding present. You'll have to take their availability into account when planning your schedule.

When will there be sales on in the shops? Plan your shopping into your schedule. If you're having a Christmas wedding, you could buy all your decorations a year ahead in the January sales and save yourself a fortune! If you wait till March you will have missed the boat.

Plan your wedding like a military procedure and you'll find it less stressful. You might find a software package helpful. Or buy a big wallchart and write everything on it.

First things first

When you first get engaged and need to start planning your wedding, the vast amount of things that you need to organize can seem daunting. Here's where to start – try to get on with these things as soon as possible.

Announce your engagement and have your party! The last thing you'll want, as a DIY bride, is to be throwing an engagement party in the middle of your preparations.

Start any diets or beauty regimes. Consider the practicality of anything you decide to do – if you

Friends with particular skills, such as cake decorating, could donate their services as their wedding gift

25

have lots of fiddly card-making to do, it might not be the wisest time to start growing your nails.

Decide on your budget. Allow plenty of time for this – you might need to do some research into how much the things you want actually cost. Then, if you find that what you want is going to take you over the amount you want to spend, you'll need to take time to discuss with your fiancé the areas where you might economize.

If you're having a religious ceremony, arrange to meet the priest or minister. If you're having a civic ceremony, book the venue. Remember things get booked up well in advance, particularly if you want a Saturday wedding in the middle of the summer. Book the venue for your reception. Again, make this a priority as even church halls can be booked up well in advance!

If you are expecting friends and family to help, talk to them as soon

One year to six months before wedding

ITEM	Who	When
Book church or registry office		
Book venue for the reception		
Choose wedding rings		
Buy or make wedding dress		
Buy or make bridesmaids' dresses		
Bake fruit cake bases		
Book caterers, or plan DIY catering		
Organize insurance		
Make or order invitations		
Make cake decorations		
Book honeymoon (unless you want a last-minute bargain)		
Start growing any plants or flowers you want for table arrangements		
Book photographer or videographer or assign the job to friends		

Six months to three months before wedding

ITEM	Who	When
Decide who will make and decorate the cake		
Decide who is providing the alcohol and organize buying in bulk to reduce costs		
Book the entertainment		
Book first-night hotel		
Book florist or start practising your floristry skills		
Buy going away outfit		
Buy groom and attendants' outfits		
Make jewellery		
Make wedding favours		
Select hymns and music and book musicians for the ceremony		
Make or order orders of service, thank you cards, place cards and other stationery		
Buy shoes (time this to coincide with seasonal sales)		

as possible to get them on board. Then draw up a list of who is doing what or use the charts on pages 26–29 to check the various jobs are being done at the right times. Don't forget the little jobs either: catering for yourselves doesn't just mean doing the food. Someone will have to set up the buffet table on the day and clean up afterwards.

Remember, the more you plan ahead, the more smoothly your plans will go! Try to get things that can be done early out of the way as soon as possible.
For example: CAKE
Mum will make three fruit bases
Auntie Jean will decorate
Cakes made by March 31st
decorated by April 30th

Three months before wedding

ITEM	Who	When
Organize gift list		
Choose or make veil and head-dress		
Arrange wedding dress fittings (if applicable)		
Organize or book your transport		
Check passports and innoculations		
Book make-up, start practising or enrol on a course of make-up lessons		
Book hairdresser or start practising!		
Reconfirm any prior bookings		

Two months before wedding

ITEM	Who	When
Check you have all accessories		
Buy presents for attendants		
Post invitations with gift list		

On the morning of your wedding, allow some time to pamper yourself and perhaps enjoy a glass of champagne!

The week of the wedding

ITEM	Who	When
Decorate the reception venue		
Add the finishing touches to the cake		
Make up flower arrangements (as late as possible)		
Have a manicure and pedicure		
Pack for your honeymoon or first night		

The day of the wedding

ITEM	Who	When
Pick up flowers and take to venue		
Pick up food and drink and take to venue		
Lay out the buffet table		
Set the tables		
Drive the bride and bridesmaids to the church		
Act as ushers		
Bring your and your fiancé's going away clothes to the venue		
Take the photographs		
Organize groups for photographs		
Clear away after the reception		
Collect table cameras from the reception		
Return any hired camera equipment, crockery or suits		

CHAPTER 4

The Stationery

Your invitations set the tone for
your whole wedding as they are
the first thing your guests see.
Here's how to have beautifully
co-ordinated stationery even on
a limited budget.

*A good place to start planning
your wedding is with the stationery*

Stationery for your wedding is perhaps the easiest place to start. First, make a list of the stationery that you want: invitations, reply cards, orders of service, menus, place cards, thank you cards and so on.

Next you need to set your budget. Bear in mind that hand-made cards are not necessarily going to be cheaper than buying conventional cards. If you're planning to use hand-made paper, miniature roses, mounting cards and ribbons, the cost will soon add up. On the other hand, it will be far cheaper than buying hand-made cards from a wedding supplier.

As an alternative to making your own stationery from scratch, you could buy ready-made invitations, which have blank insides so that you can fill in the gaps. Bear in mind that filling in your names and the date, time and venue of your wedding might not take long if you're doing one invitation, but it could take hours to carefully fill in a hundred.

You could also buy notelets and print the inserts yourselves on a computer. You can buy packs of cards very cheaply. Look in bargain bookstores as well as conventional stationers. Simply glue your inserts in with a little PVA glue.

Wording the invitations

TRADITIONAL

Mr and Mrs Fred Bloggs request the pleasure of

....

*at the marriage of their daughter Ann
to Mr John Smith*

ALTERNATIVE WORDINGS

Bridal couple as hosts

*Miss Ann Bloggs
and Mr John Smith
request the pleasure of*

....

at their marriage

Remarried mother/father as hosts

*Mr and Mrs Fred Bloggs
and Mr and Mrs Tim Hill request the pleasure of*

....

*at the marriage
of their daughter Ann to Mr John Smith*

Widowed mother as host

*Mrs Fred Bloggs requests
the pleasure of*

....

*at the marriage
of her daughter Ann
to Mr John Smith*

Divorced parents as hosts

*Mr Fred Bloggs
and Mrs Sarah Jones
request the pleasure of*

....

*at the marriage of their
daughter Ann
to Mr John Smith*

33

To make a considerable saving on both materials and postage, create an electronic version of your invitations or thank you cards and email them.

If you do want to make your own stationery, you'll need a design. Not inspired? Not creative? Then copy! Have a look at hand-made cards in your local shop, try classes at your local craft shop, base your design around a motif cut from wedding gift wrap or use one of the template designs on pages 39, 43, 44 and 46.

Once you've got your design, time yourself making one card. If it takes you an hour and you need to make a hundred invitations, not to mention orders of service, place cards, thank you cards and so on, you will need to give up your day job! Stick to a design you can make in a reasonable amount of time.

All the materials used to make the cards in this book are readily available from good stationers and craft shops.

As an alternative to making your own cards from scratch, buy notelets and insert your printed message

Mr. and Mrs. William Page request the honour of your company at the marriage of their daughter Jennifer to Mr. Neil Hopkin on Saturday 3rd July at 2 p.m. at Ealing Green Methodist Church.

*You can purchase all the materials
used to make the cards in this book
from stationers and craft shops*

Bridal Bouquet Invitations

You will need:

- ♥ Blank cards and envelopes
- ♥ Glue (PVA/vinyl)
- ♥ Small flowers
- ♥ Wide sheer ribbon or voile
- ♥ Hand-made paper in complementary colour
- ♥ Thin ribbon
- ♥ 'Invitation' sticker sheet
- ♥ Craft knife, scissors, ruler, pencil

2 Take a 2½in (6cm) strip of your voile ribbon or a 2½ x 1¼in (6 x 3cm) rectangle of voile and wrap around your flowers to make a bouquet. Secure with a bow made from thin ribbon.

3 Take your hand-made paper and measure out approximately 2½in (6cm) to make a frame for your bouquet. Fold to score then tear.

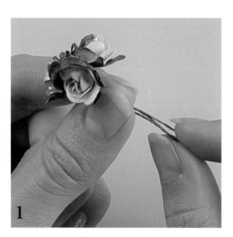

1 Take three of the flowers, cut the stems to approximately 1in (2.5cm) and twist them together.

4 Using clear PVA glue, fix the square of hand-made paper onto the card, and then fix the bouquet onto the square.

5 From your sticker sheet, peel off the word 'invitation' and mount onto a small rectangle of card. You might find it helpful to use an embroidery needle or cocktail stick to transfer the sticker from the sheet to the card. For best results, cut the rectangle from the same card that you are using as your card base.

6 Mount this small rectangle of card on a second slightly bigger rectangle torn from your hand-made paper and fix the rectangle underneath the bouquet using PVA glue.

7 Print out the inserts giving details of the time and place of your ceremony and reception. Cut to size and glue into your card with PVA glue.

A quick and cheap alternative to the flower bouquet, is to mount a motif cut from gift wrap. This will look more effective if double-mounted onto two co-ordinating squares of hand-made paper (see card laying down in the picture on page 35). Alternatively, use a photograph of your marriage venue as your motif – you could even modify the image on your computer!

Sequins Wedding Cake

You will need:

- ♥ 3 different varieties of silver wedding confetti
- ♥ Card bases and envelopes
- ♥ Blank overhead projector transparencies
- ♥ Sequins
- ♥ Glue (PVA/vinyl)
- ♥ Silver permanent marker
- ♥ Scissors
- ♥ 'Invitation' sticker sheet
- ♥ Scissors, ruler, tweezers, cocktail stick or needle

1 Cut a 1¾ x 2in (4.5 x 5cm) rectangle from the transparency.

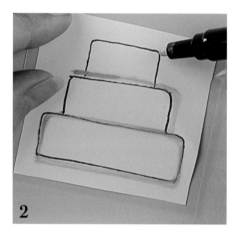

2

2 Using the silver marker and the wedding cake template from page 39, trace the outline of the cake onto the transparency.

3

3 Glue four sequins on the bottom layer of the cake, three on the next layer, two on the top layer and one on top of the cake. You might find it helpful to use tweezers for this. Don't overdo the glue or it will make the transparency appear dirty.

4 Put a dab of PVA glue on each corner of the transparency and press onto the card base.

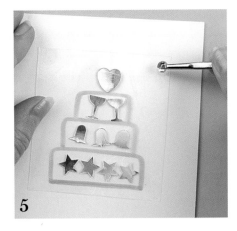

5

5 Take four sequins. Put a dab of glue on the back of each and place on top of the transparency, concealing the glue mark where it is stuck to the card base.

6 From your sticker sheet, peel off the words 'Wedding invitation' and mount on the card underneath the cake. Print out the inserts giving details of your wedding and glue into your card with PVA glue.

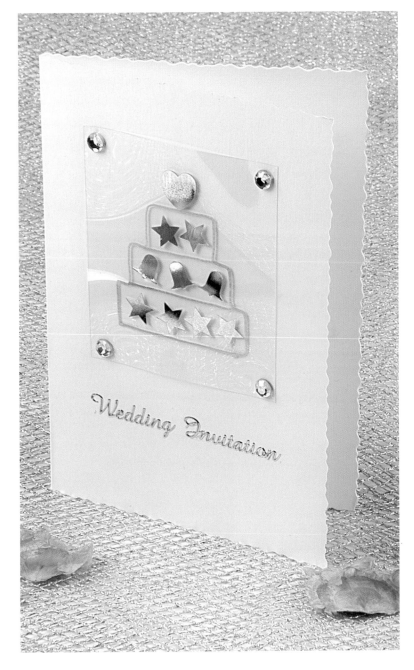

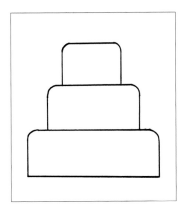

Wedding cake template

Beaded Heart

You will need:

♥ Thin hand-made paper
♥ Jewellery wire
♥ Small pearl beads
♥ Glue (PVA/vinyl)
♥ Card bases and envelopes
♥ Wire cutters, ruler

1 Take your hand-made paper and measure out a square with sides of approximately ¾in (2cm). Fold to score then tear.

You could make more of these hearts to decorate the stems of wine glasses at your reception.

2 Using your fingers, gently tease the sides of the square until the edges fray. When you are happy with the result, fix the square to your base card using a small amount of PVA glue.

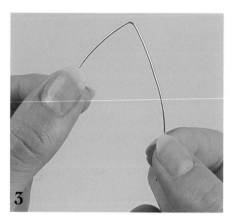

3

3 Take a 3½in (9cm) length of the jewellery wire. Bend it into a point approximately 1¼in (3cm) from one end.

4 Continue bending the wire until you have made a heart shape, with the ends of wire meeting in the middle. One end will be longer than the other. Twist the wire *once* to keep the ends together.

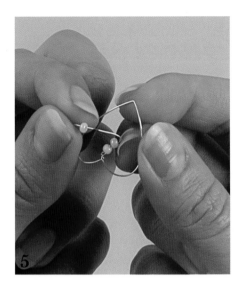

5 Thread the longer end of the wire with six pearl beads. Bend round to make a loop in the centre of the heart. Then twist with the other end of wire to keep the beads in place. Thread any loose wire back through the beads.

6 Using a small amount of PVA glue, fix the wire heart onto the hand-made paper frame on the card base. Attach the printed insert giving details of your wedding as required.

Invitation Card and Envelope

You will need:

- ♥ Card bases and envelopes
- ♥ Wedding invitation sticker sheets
- ♥ Glue (PVA/vinyl)

- ♥ Card in 2 contrasting shades
- ♥ Scissors, pencil, ruler, cocktail stick

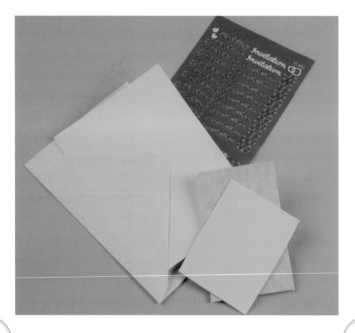

1 Cut out an envelope shape in one shade of card using the template on page 43. Fold this into an envelope shape, using PVA glue to fix. To save time, you could use miniature envelopes, which you can buy ready-made from good craft shops.

2 Cut a 1⅔ x 1½in (4 x 3.5cm) rectangle from the other shade of card and fold in half. Peel off the word 'invitation' from the sticker sheet and mount onto this rectangle. You may find it easiest to transfer the sticker from the sheet to the card using a cocktail stick or thick needle. Alternatively, you could print out the words 'wedding invitation' several times on a sheet of card using your home computer and then cut them out.

3 Place the miniature invitation card inside the miniature envelope and glue in place.

4 Stick the miniature envelope onto the base card using PVA glue. Insert details of your wedding as required.

Variation

♥

Add a single stem
flower.
Curve the stem to make
a graceful sweep across
the card and fix in
place with
PVA glue.

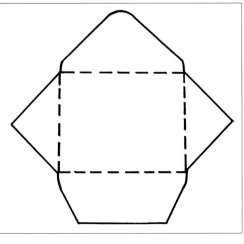

*Cut along the straight
lines of the template
(left) and fold along
the dotted lines to
make your miniature
envelope*

Foil Heart

You will need:

- ♥ Thick craft foil
- ♥ Wedding invitation stickers
- ♥ Glue (PVA/vinyl)
- ♥ Card bases and envelopes
- ♥ Pencil, scissors, ruler, cocktail stick

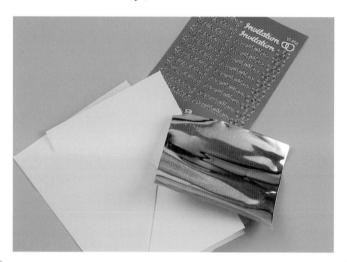

the pencil, mark your design on the wrong side of the foil. You can make up your own design or use the template below.

1 Cut out a rectangle, 1¼ x 1½in (3 x 3.5cm), from the foil.

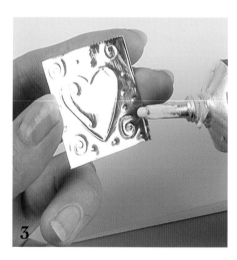

3 Mount the foil onto the card using PVA glue.

2 Place the foil upside down on a soft surface such as a magazine. Using

4 Peel off the word 'wedding' from your sticker sheet and, using a cocktail stick or needle, place above the foil rectangle on the card. Press down. Stick another 'wedding' underneath the foil. This should be placed upside down. Peel off the word 'invitation' and stick down the right-hand edge of the foil. Peel off a second 'invitation' and place this running up along the left-hand edge of the foil.

5 Insert the printed details of your wedding as required.

Glass Painting

You will need:

- ♥ Glue (PVA/vinyl)
- ♥ Gold card bases and envelopes
- ♥ Glass paint outliner in gold
- ♥ Glass paint in red and green
- ♥ Blank overhead projector transparencies or thick perpex sheets from a craft shop
- ♥ Gold wedding invitation stickers
- ♥ Cream card
- ♥ Craft knife, paintbrush, ruler, scissors

Follow this template for your glass painting or do your own design

1 Using the craft knife and a ruler, cut out a 1¾in (4.5cm) square of acetate or perspex sheet. The perspex sheet is thicker and will give your glass painting more of a 3-D feel.

2 Place the square of perspex on the template (left), or on a design of your own, and trace using the glass outliner. Keep a steady pressure on the tube of outliner so that you get lines of even thickness. You might need to practise this several times! Leave to dry.

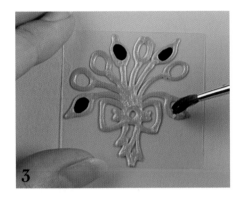

edges of the outliner. If this does happen, use a cotton bud to mop up any excess paint.

4 In a similar way, fill in the flowers and the bow with red glass paint. When the paint is dry, mount the glass painting onto the base card. From your sticker sheet, peel off the words 'wedding invitation' and mount onto a small rectangle of cream-coloured card. Mount this under the glass painting. Fix the printed insert giving details of your wedding into the card using PVA glue.

3 When the outliner has dried, fill in the leaf shapes using green glass paint and a very fine paintbrush. Do not overload the paintbrush with paint or the paint will spill over the raised

You could paint your design onto wine glasses for an ultra-co-ordinated look at your reception. Just be careful how you wash them afterwards!

Alternative Painting Design

You will need:
- ♥ Glue (PVA/vinyl)
- ♥ Pale blue or pale pink card bases and envelopes
- ♥ Glass paint outliner in silver
- ♥ Glass paint in pale blue and pink
- ♥ Small mirror tiles
- ♥ Silver wedding invitation stickers
- ♥ White card
- ♥ Paintbrush, ruler, scissors

1 Take three mirror tiles and using outliner, draw a heart on one, a star on another and a horseshoe on the third. When dry, paint the heart pink and the other two blue.

2 Mount the mirror tiles vertically on a long strip of white card. Finish off with the words 'Wedding invitation', also mounted on white card, and don't forget to insert the details of your wedding!

Orders of Service

Any of the invitation designs in this chapter can be easily adapted for your order of service. Just use bigger base cards.

There is often confusion about what needs to go inside the order of service. Remember that it is just there to give your guests an idea of your running order and to enable them to participate in the ceremony as appropriate e.g. by singing hymns.

As for the running order itself, there are many different ways of actually structuring your wedding. If you are having a religious ceremony, you will find it helpful to discuss the order of service with your minister. Alongside the marriage ceremony itself, most people have one or two readings, an address, prayers and a blessing and two hymns. However it's your day so, with your minister's agreement, it is important to make it what you want. Page 50 gives suggested running orders for both a religious and a non-religious ceremony – remember they're intended just as guides.

You can adapt any of the invitation designs in this chapter for your order of service

Order of Service

SUGGESTED WORDING FOR A RELIGIOUS CEREMONY

Title and composer of the music for the bride's arrival

•

Welcome – include the minister's name

•

First hymn – include the words of the hymn, not just the title so that your congregation can sing along

•

The marriage

•

Reading – include the title/source of the extract and the name of the reader

•

The address

•

Second hymn – again, don't forget to include all the words

•

The prayers

•

The signing of the registers – don't forget to include the title of the music, composer and performer that will entertain your guests whilst you do this

•

The blessing

•

Recessional – include the title of the music and the composer

NON-RELIGIOUS CEREMONY

The arrival of the bride – include the music's title and its composer

•

Introduction and welcome – include the name of the celebrant

•

Reading – include the title and source of the extract and the name of the reader

•

The ceremony

•

The exchange of rings

•

The signing of the register

•

The recessional – include the title of the music and the composer

Additional Stationery

The invitation designs can also be adapted to make other items of stationery, so that your wedding is beautifully co-ordinated.

For example, you might want matching menus and place cards at your reception. You could also make your own thank you cards.

Place cards are obviously much smaller than invitations so you might need to adapt the design to fit! For example, if you've used the alternative glass painting design with three mirror tiles on each invitation, just use one mirror tile on your place card.

CHAPTER 5

The Catering

Whether it's an intimate family
gathering or an enormous party
you're after, here are some ideas
for how to have a dream
reception on a nightmare budget!

Doing the catering for your own wedding is a huge undertaking. However, unless you have a huge budget to spend on caterers, you might find that DIY is the best way to get the food you'd like on a limited budget.

Before my wedding, the most my husband-to-be and I had ever catered for was a dinner party for six people. But we managed to do a sumptuous cold buffet for 90 people and, with hindsight, could probably have done it for far less than we actually spent. Doing your own catering will also save you money on

We managed to put together a sumptuous cold buffet for 90 people

alcohol – you can buy your own and not pay anyone corkage!

Hints and tips

♥ Storing your food properly is important, unless you want everybody to go down with food poisoning! If you get everything laid out on large platters before the ceremony, you'll need lots of room in your fridge to fit them in! Depending on the numbers you are catering for, buy one or more second-hand fridges for your venue. You might be able to sell them back to the shop after the wedding. If not, advertise them in your local paper. If you're going straight off on your honeymoon, remember to arrange for a friend to pick them up and do this.
♥ Make sure that food is covered until just before it's served. Buy plenty of plastic food wrap!
♥ Look in your local telephone directory for places to hire crockery, cutlery and tablecloths. You can sometimes even return the crockery unwashed if you pay a little extra! Think carefully about what you'll need – it's easy to forget the little things like teaspoons and then find you're short when it comes to serving tea and coffee after the meal.
♥ You'll need a team of helpers. Find out if any friends are willing to make dishes in advance. You'll definitely need people for the morning of the big day itself to get the food to the venue while you are getting ready, as well as collecting any pre-ordered

food. Once at the venue the food will need to be arranged on platters, ready to serve. On a hot day, they'll need to put it all into the fridges to keep fresh. Just after the ceremony, the team will need to lay everything out on the buffet table. And afterwards they will need to pack everything away. Even if you're sending your hired crockery back to the shop unwashed, it will still take time to pack all those plates, knives and forks into boxes.

♥ Think about the logistics of where everything is going to go in your venue. How big is the food preparation area? Where will the guests' dirty plates go when they have finished their main course and want to get started on the desserts?

If your friends associate a certain food with you – perhaps you're fanatical about sausage sandwiches or can't live without lime pickle – why not feature that on your menu?

Alternative solutions

If you can't afford caterers and don't want to cater for yourself, here are a few ideas for cost-effective food with a difference:

♥ Get everyone to bring a dish to share!

♥ Have a barbecue. Recruit a team of helpers to be in charge on the day.

♥ Ask your favourite take-away restaurant if they will provide a buffet for you.

♥ Take over a restaurant. This can be cheaper than you expect, especially if you choose to have your wedding on a day when the restaurant is quiet. Arrange in advance how many drinks you'll be paying for.

♥ Have a picnic and get your guests to bring hampers.

♥ Serve champagne, trays of canapés and strawberries. Organize helpers in advance to pass these around and make it obvious on the invitations that you won't be serving a full meal.

♥ Have afternoon tea. Order plates of sandwiches, delicious cakes and clotted cream scones for that luxurious touch.

Hiring out a whole restaurant can be cheaper than you might expect

♥ Lots of shops produce ready-made party food. You'll find selections of mini quiches and other finger buffet food in most supermarkets. Try asking at your local delicatessen about what they might be able to provide. Many will be happy to supply mixed platters of party foods or plenty of sliced cold meats for much less than you would pay a professional caterer.

♥ Keep it simple. Fancy garnishes are great for a dinner party of six but impossible if you are an amateur catering for 100!

♥ Unless you have a talented friend who can do the catering for you, the only practical option is to have a cold buffet. For hot food you'd need masses of oven space, helpers prepared to miss out on the actual ceremony to heat everything up and lots of culinary skills!

♥ Have trays of canapés and drinks ready to pass round immediately – this will buy your team of helpers a little time if they aren't quite ready with the buffet table.

♥ Remember you'll need plenty of platters for cold meats and quiche and large bowls of salad. You can buy disposable platters in lots of supermarkets. If you prefer, these can be disguised under a bed of exotic salad leaves. In the summer, supermarkets also sell large plastic salad bowls – they're designed for picnics but they are inexpensive, look good and do the job!

♥ Don't forget the serving utensils. Try supermarkets for a range of reasonably priced salad tongs and serving spoons.

♥ It is helpful to vegetarians and people with food allergies if you label your food.

♥ Keep a separate table for cutlery, napkins and bread, and another one for desserts. You might even consider having two separate but identical main buffet tables to save time on queuing.

♥ Make it clear what your guests are going to get so that no-one is disappointed. For example, if you clearly state on your invitation that the wedding ceremony will be followed by 'an informal buffet reception from 3.30 till 6.30 in the church hall', nobody will arrive expecting cordon bleu with silver service, followed by an all-night disco. You don't want to have disappointed guests!

♥ Is anyone going to serve the food at your wedding or will it be completely self-service? If it is self-service, you'll have to make it obvious. Guests will also need to know where to put their empty plates when they've finished the main course so they can go and choose their dessert. A few waiters and waitresses might make things easier if you are able to organize some. You might consider paying any teenage cousins or their friends to do the job.

Choosing your menu

Unless you are an accomplished cook and used to throwing big parties, doing your own catering is a daunting task! But the key is in the planning and planning begins with choosing your menu.

The possibilities for your menu are limitless. Choose food that will suit you and your guests. There's a sample buffet menu on page 58 to give you an idea of what can be done. Copy it, adapt it or ignore it altogether and go for whatever food you like!

If you have a lot of vegetarians you will need to make sure you cater adequately for them. You could choose a themed menu such as a Mexican or Indian buffet. If there are a lot of children at your wedding, you should include plenty of food that will appeal to them and be easy for them to eat. If you are having a finger buffet, you'll need to choose foods that are easy to eat standing up, preferably without a knife and fork.

It is a well-known fact that presentation of food is all-important. It's not just about how you present your food on the buffet table but also how you present it on your menu: 'roast topside of beef' sounds a lot more appealing than 'cold beef'! It is also best to avoid the word 'small' in reference to food, but the words 'cocktail' and 'miniature' make it sound chic rather than inadequate! It's better to describe your salads as 'fresh coleslaw' and

If you are having a finger buffet choose foods that are easy to eat standing up

'new potato and mint salad' than just plain old 'coleslaw' and 'potato salad'. It might not have been labelled so temptingly in its supermarket tub, but your guests are less likely to notice!

Plan your menu around what you can easily do and what help you will have. If you don't have a lot of people to assist you, you'll need a very simple menu.

Remember that unless you want to break with tradition and see your groom on the morning of the wedding, you can't both be in the reception venue setting out the food.

In any case, most brides are more focused on their own appearance than that of their buffet table on the morning of their wedding, so it is wise to delegate the job of setting out the buffet tables.

Smoked salmon canapés with assorted fillings
Cocktail vol-au-vents with cream of mushroom

Whole poached salmon
Roast topside of beef
Honey roast ham
Traditional pork pie topped with cranberries
Duck paté with port wine

A selection of vegetarian quiches

New potato and mint salad
Fresh coleslaw
Mixed green salad
A selection of freshly baked rolls

Rich chocolate torte
Traditional baked cheesecake
Strawberries and cream

Cheese platter

Tea or coffee

Sample buffet menu

If the sample menu shown on page 58 seems difficult, the following pages explain how to put it together. You don't need amazing culinary skills, just careful planning and organization and a reliable, hard-working team of helpers.

The canapés

You can order large trays of canapés from many supermarkets. If you can't find a supermarket that offers this, buy plenty of smoked salmon and soft cheese. Mix the soft cheese with a variety of different herbs or, for even quicker results, buy soft cheese that is already flavoured. Spread the cheese on a slice of smoked salmon, roll into a sausage shape and slice into canapés. For the vol-au-vents, buy ready-to-bake vol-au-vent cases and fill either with tins of creamed mushroom or make your own creamed mushrooms by cooking lots of mushrooms in a little white wine with some garlic and adding cream or crème fraiche.

The main courses

Once again, see what you can order from your local supermarket. Failing this, try your local delicatessen. They should be able to supply you with large platters of sliced meats. See what else they have on offer that would add that extra special luxurious touch to your buffet table, for example, large pork pies covered in cranberries or luxurious patés. Use and be inspired by what you

Many wine merchants offer free glass hire with your purchase

can find locally. You can buy whole salmon from your supermarket or fishmonger and poach and dress these yourself. Vegetarian quiche is easy and cheap to make. You can buy or make your pastry cases, make a large quantity of basic quiche mixture – you'll need lots of eggs for this – and then fill each one with something different such as mushrooms or broccoli and cheese.

The bread

Again, use what you can find locally. Ask the best baker in your area to provide a selection of different rolls. Of course, you could buy a huge mound of white rolls from the super-market, but a selection of different

A good sparkling wine is a cost-effective alternative to champagne

types of bread won't be any more work for you and will help give your buffet table the professional touch. If you buy French sticks, they'll need to be sliced at the very last minute to ensure they don't go hard.

The salads

You could ask friends and family to help by making the salads: coleslaw, potato salad and green salads are all easy to prepare. Alternatively, try your local cash and carry and buy large catering packs. A few sprigs of fresh parsley and mint will add a home-made touch.

The desserts

When you order your bread, ask your baker what desserts he can provide. Large chocolate tortes or cheesecakes can add a sumptuous touch to the dessert table. Add a mountain of strawberries – either from the supermarket or ask friends to go to a pick-your-own farm a couple of days before the wedding – and don't forget the large jug of double cream. Your local delicatessen should also be able to provide you with a variety of cheeses. Finally, if you're intending to serve tea and coffee after the meal, and your buffet is self-service, you'll need to find someone to organize this for you.

Calculating quantities

Unless you're a caterer, this is one of the most difficult things about doing your own catering. Here are some tips to help you get it right:

♥ Not having enough food would be embarrassing! However, as you're catering yourself, you can afford to err on the overgenerous side with your quantities. Work out what to do with any leftovers so that you don't have to see them go to waste.

♥ Not everyone will want every food on your buffet table. The people that have second helpings of coleslaw will be balanced out by the people that don't have any at all. If you're having six different types of salad, you won't need as much of each as if you were only having three types of salad. Imagine how much one person can put on their plate if they have a small amount of everything and base your calculations on that. Just because your little brother will eat five chicken drumsticks, does not mean you need to allow five chicken drumsticks for every guest.

♥ Take the advice of your delicatessen or baker. If they say that their large cheesecake and their large chocolate torte will each feed 12, trust them. If you were having 60 guests, you'd therefore need five cakes for everyone to have one slice of one of the cakes. Don't assume that everyone will want a slice of each and buy five of each cake. Equally, don't assume that no-one will want one of each or a second slice of one. Strike a happy medium and allow a little extra.

If you choose caterers

♥ If you do decide to use caterers, a cold finger buffet will work out cheaper than a hot sit-down meal. Again, it might be a good idea to indicate that the reception will be informal so that your guests know what to expect.

♥ Clarify with the caterers in advance what each guest will be entitled to – even the suavest venue has been known to count out strawberries for each guest.

♥ Don't have both hors d'oeuvres and a starter. Choose either one or the other. If you do want a starter, soup will be a cheaper option and is generally more widely popular as well!

♥ Choose just one main meal option that everyone will like, and make sure you don't forget to include a vegetarian option.

♥ Have your wedding cake as your dessert. These days you can even buy chocolate wedding cakes!

You could have your wedding cake as your dessert

Drinks

♥ If you're supplying your own alcohol, remember that many caterers and venues charge corkage – this is a surcharge on every bottle that you drink. Try to negotiate a flat fee for corkage or a per-head fee if you think that you and your guests will consume a lot!

♥ Choose a good sparkling wine instead of champagne. Alternatively, have Buck's Fizz to make your champagne go further or add a scoop of sorbet to your sparkling wine for a delicious 'ice-cream soda'.

♥ Negotiate a discount by buying in bulk from a wine warehouse.

♥ If your reception is at a pub or hotel, make sure everyone has at least one drink. Then have a paying bar. This is perfectly acceptable.

♥ Many wine merchants will allow you free glass hire with your purchase.

♥ Try to buy your wine on a sale or return basis. Remember to organize a friend to pick any leftovers up after the wedding and take them back for you. Leave them at the venue and you might not see them again!

♥ As a general guide, allow at least half a bottle of wine per person. If you have bought your wine on sale or return, allowing extra will be no problem.

♥ Don't forget the soft drinks!

♥ For the toast, aim to get about seven or eight glasses from each bottle of champagne.

♥ Finally, if your venue is taking care of the wine for you, it might be sensible to impose an upper limit.

CHAPTER 6

The Wedding Cake

Whether you want a traditional
three-tiered fruit cake or a more
modern chocolate extravaganza,
this chapter will show you how
you can have your cake and eat it!

This is something that, whilst not easy to make, you can have a go at well in advance. Fruit cake actually improves with age and if it goes wrong you'll still have plenty of time to have another go or order one from a professional!

Before you decide to go ahead and make your own cake, add up the costs. The ingredients for a fruit cake are expensive but, unless you already do a lot of baking, you'll also need to buy all the equipment: a large mixing bowl, scales, cake tins for each tier, large containers for storage, cake boards, icing smoothers, rolling pin and board, tools for making sugar roses and so on. This can make the whole project very expensive. If making your own cake is something you are doing just in order to save money, it might be cheaper to buy ready-iced cakes from a supermarket and decorate them yourself (see 'Alternatives to making your own cake', below). If you've never baked a fruit cake before, bake a small one first. Dried fruit isn't cheap. If you like what you've made, have a go for real.

Alternatives to making your own cake

♥ If you don't want to make the cake yourself, why not buy ready-made tiers from a supermarket? You can decorate these using the ideas in this chapter.

♥ If you can't bake but want to have a go at icing and decorating, find out if there is a local baker who would be willing to make the cake bases for you.

♥ Or if you can bake but want a more professional look for the finished cake, ask at your local sugarcraft shop if they do an icing service for cakes you've made.

♥ Instead of a traditional wedding cake, make a huge pile of fairy cakes. You won't be able to cut the cake together, but you could share the top cake!

You can make and ice up cakes well in advance

Traditional Fruit Cake

You will need:

For a 18in (46cm) round or a 16in (40½cm) square cake

- ♥ 14oz (400gms) currants
- ♥ 9oz (250gms) sultanas
- ♥ 5½oz (150gms) raisins
- ♥ 3½oz (100gms) glacé cherries
- ♥ 2½oz (70gms) mixed peel
- ♥ 1 lemon
- ♥ 3 tbsp brandy

- ♥ 9oz (250gms) plain flour
- ♥ 1½ tsp ground mixed spice
- ♥ ½ tsp ground nutmeg
- ♥ 7oz (200gms) soft margarine
- ♥ 8oz (225gms) light muscovado sugar
- ♥ 1 tbsp black treacle
- ♥ 5 beaten eggs

(For quantities for alternative sizes, see chart on page 68)

1 Grease a deep, 18in (46cm) round cake tin. Line the base and sides with a double thickness of greaseproof paper and grease the paper.

2 Preheat the oven to Gas Mark 1 or 140°C.

3 Chop the glacé cherries and wash the fruit. Grate the lemon rind and discard the rest of the lemon. Then put all the ingredients in a large bowl and mix them up. It's as easy as that!

You'll probably be mixing for a good ten minutes, especially if working with larger quantities. This can be quite hard work so you might want to consider mixing the ingredients for your larger tiers in two batches or enlist the help of your husband-to-be!

4 Spoon the mixture into your lined and greased tin. Flatten with the back of a large spoon. Aim to make the top of the cake slightly concave.

5 Bake for around three hours. To test if the cake is ready, insert a skewer into the centre. It should come out clean if the cake is done.

6 When the cake has cooled remove it from the tin. Leave the lining paper on the cake until you are ready to put on the marzipan to keep it moist. Store in an airtight container in a cool place.

QUANTITIES

ROUND CAKE TIN	$7^7/8$in (20cm)	9in (23cm)	$9^7/8$in (25cm)	11in (28cm)	$11^3/4$in (30cm)
SQUARE CAKE TIN	$7^1/8$in (18cm)	$7^7/8$in (20cm)	9in (23cm)	$9^7/8$in (25cm)	11in (28cm)
Currants	$17^3/4$oz (500gms)	21ozs (600gms)	$24^3/4$oz (700gms)	$28^1/4$oz (800gms)	$33^1/2$oz (950gms)
Sultanas	$10^1/2$oz (300gms)	$13^1/4$oz (375gms)	16oz (450gms)	$19^1/2$oz (550gms)	21oz (600gms)
Raisins	$6^1/4$oz (175gms)	7oz (200gms)	8oz (225gms)	$8^3/4$oz (250gms)	$8^3/4$oz (250gms)
Glacé cherries	$4^1/2$oz (125gms)	$5^1/4$oz (150gms)	$6^1/4$oz (175gms)	7oz (200gms)	7oz (200gms)
Mixed peel	3oz (90gms)	$4^1/4$oz (120gms)	$5^1/4$oz (150gms)	$6^1/2$oz (180gms)	7oz (200gms)
Lemons	2	2	2	3	3
Brandy	4 tbsp	4 tbsp	5 tbsp	6 tbsp	6 tbsp
Plain flour	$10^1/2$oz (300gms)	14ozs (400gms)	16oz (450gms)	$19^1/2$oz (550gms)	22oz (625gms)
Ground mixed spice	$1^1/2$tsp	$1^1/2$tsp	2 tsp	$2^1/2$tsp	3 tsp
Ground nutmeg	1 tsp	1 tsp	$1^1/2$tsp	$1^1/2$tsp	2 tsp
Soft margarine	$8^3/4$oz (250gms)	$10^1/2$oz (300gms)	$13^1/4$oz (375gms)	15oz (425gms)	$17^3/4$oz (500gms)
Light muscovado sugar	$9^3/4$oz (275gms)	$12^1/2$oz (350gms)	14oz (400gms)	16oz (450gms)	$17^3/4$oz (500gms)
Black treacle	$1^1/2$tsp	2 tbsp	2 tbsp	$2^1/2$tbsp	$2^1/2$tbsp
Eggs	6	7	8	9	10
BAKING TIME	$3^1/2$hrs	4hrs	$4^1/2$hrs	5hrs	$5^1/2$hrs
PORTIONS	38	50	64	80	115

Making a Madeira Cake

Not everybody likes fruit cake so you might want to have an alternative, perhaps just for the top tier of your cake.

You will need:

- ♥ 10½oz (300gms) self-raising flour
- ♥ 3½oz (100gms) plain flour
- ♥ 8¾oz (250gms) soft margarine
- ♥ 8¾oz (250gms) caster sugar
- ♥ 4 eggs
- ♥ 1½ tsp lemon juice

Quantities given here are for a 7⅛in (18cm) round cake. For larger sizes add more eggs and work out the quantities in proportion. Remember to allow a little longer for baking.

1 Preheat the oven to 160°C or Gas Mark 3.

2 Grease an 7⅛in (18cm) round cake tin. Line with a double thickness of greaseproof paper and grease the paper.

3 Cream the sugar and margarine in a bowl.

4 Beat the eggs and add them one at a time with a spoonful of sifted flour. Mix thoroughly.

5 Gently fold in the rest of the flour and the lemon juice.

6 Spoon the mixture into your greased and lined tin and bake for approximately one and a half hours. You can insert a skewer into the centre of the cake to test if it is ready – if the skewer comes out clean, the cake is done. If the top of the cake begins to brown too quickly, cover it with foil.

7

7 Let the cake cool thoroughly before turning out. Madeira cakes will normally rise slightly and the top will crack. You can slice the top off prior to icing in order to get a flat surface.

There's no law that says all your tiers have to be the same. Why not have two tiers of fruit cake and one of madeira sponge for any guests who don't like fruit?

Covering a Cake with Marzipan

1 If the cake is not flat, fill any hollows with a little marzipan. If the top is higher than the edges, it's helpful to build up the edges too. If your cake is very domed, you might want to slice off the dome to give yourself a flat surface to work with. Tip the cake upside down so that the base becomes the top.

2 Brush the cake with a little apricot jam. Sieve this first in order to get rid of the apricot pieces or remove them with a spoon.

3 Dust your work surface with icing sugar. Knead your marzipan until it is soft then roll it into a ball. Roll out the marzipan until it is about 5mm thick. It should be large enough to cover the top and sides of the cake in one piece.

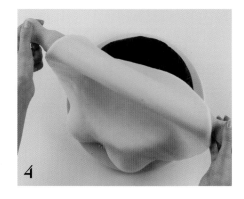

4 Using the rolling pin, lift the marzipan from the work surface to the cake and place it over the top. Smooth the top surface with your hand to get rid of any air bubbles.

5 Smooth the marzipan down the sides of the cake, ensuring there are no creases. Keep trimming the excess away at the base of the cake.

6 With the palm of your hand or an icing smoother, smooth all the surfaces. Then leave the cake to dry for at least 12 hours before covering it with sugarpaste icing.

You can buy marzipan at specialist cake shops that looks and tastes like it's home-made!

Covering a Cake with Sugarpaste Icing

Sugarpaste icing is easier than royal icing. You can make your own, buy it in the supermarket or buy it from a specialist sugarcraft shop. Making your own is cheapest but I find I get best results by buying it from a specialist shop.

Note: If your cake is fruit, then it needs to be covered with marzipan first (see page 70). If it's sponge, you can cover it with sugarpaste icing straightaway.

2 Dust your work surface with icing sugar and roll out the sugarpaste to about a ⅛in (0.5cm) thickness so it is large enough to cover the entire cake.

3 Just as you did with your marzipan, use the rolling pin to transfer the icing to the cake. Place the icing on top of the cake so that it falls evenly down each side.

1 Brush the marzipan with a little water to help the sugarpaste stick.

The quantities given below are intended as a guide to how much marzipan and sugarpaste icing you should buy. The amounts given are quite generous, as if you buy too little and have to roll your icing too thinly, it will make it more difficult to ice your cake.

Round cake	7⅞in (20cm)	9in (23cm)	9¾in (25cm)	11in (28cm)	11¾in (30cm)
Square cake	7⅛in (18cm)	7⅞in (20cm)	9in (23cm)	9¾in (25cm)	11in (28cm)
Quantity of marzipan/sugarpaste icing required(1250gms)	17¾oz (500gms)	23¾oz (675gms)	31¾oz (900gms)	35¼oz (1kg)	44oz

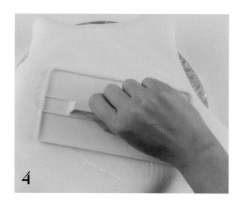

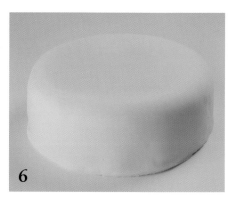

4 Rub your hands with a little corn-flour to prevent the icing sticking to them, then smooth the top surface to get rid of any air bubbles. You could also use an icing smoother for this.

5 Smooth the sides of the cake, getting rid of any creases and air bubbles.

6 Trim off any excess icing at the base of the cake.

7 Transfer the cake to a cake board. It's easier to pick the cake up if you slide it to the edge of a work surface so you can get your hand underneath!

Presenting your Cake

Using pillars

If you're going to use pillars to stack your cake, you'll need to transport each tier separately and assemble your cake at the venue.

The best sort of cake to stack this way is a fruit cake. If you're having mixed tiers, you can put a sponge cake as your top tier, but don't make the mistake of trying to stack a fruit cake on top of a sponge cake; the sponge will simply be too light to support the heavy fruit.

If you want three tiers but don't have enough guests to eat that much, buy a fake cake base. These are made of polystyrene, but you can ice them with sugarpaste and use them as one of your tiers, and nobody will know the difference.

1 Start with the bottom tier of the cake. Measure its depth. Depending on how many pillars you want, you need to cut three or four pieces of 5mm thick dowel to the depth of the cake plus the height of the pillar.

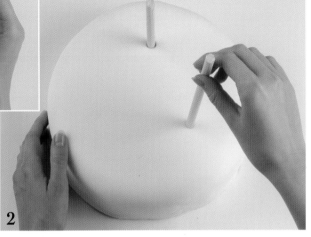

2 Insert the dowel pieces vertically into the cake. Each dowel should be about halfway between the edge and the centre of the cake.

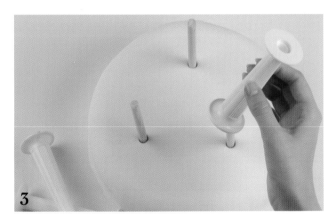

3 Place each pillar over the dowel rod and place the next tier of cake, still on its cake board, on the top! If there is another tier to go on top of this, you might find it easier to insert the dowel into the second tier before stacking the cakes.

Alternatives

If you daren't stack your cakes up on pillars, you could hire a cake stand from a specialist shop. Alternatively you could stack your cakes on top of each other without pillars. If you choose this last option, the top tier(s) should be on cake boards that are the same size as the cake. Leave the cake board on the bottom of each tier to make them easy to separate and cut. You can cover the boards with icing or ribbon so that they can't be seen.

Decorating your Cake

If you've never done it before, decorating a wedding cake can seem complicated at first. So where do you start?

There are three ideas in this book, all of which a beginner should be able to attempt. You can of course think up variations of these to suit your wedding. Collect pictures of cakes from magazines for inspiration. Look in cake shops too – there's no charge for window shopping. Adapt and simplify what you see.

Find a specialist shop which will stock everything you need and be a source of advice – look in your local telephone directory or at the listings in the back of specialist sugarcraft magazines.

You can buy sugarpaste flowers ready-made, make your own (see page 75) or use real flowers (check they aren't poisonous first!). Scattering real flowers and petals over your cake is another cheap but pretty way to decorate it.

Decorating your cake with real flowers is a cheap and pretty option

Making Sugar Roses

You will need:

- ♥ 24 gauge wires from a sugarcraft shop
- ♥ Cooled, boiled water
- ♥ Flower paste in your chosen colour (NB: this is *not* the same as the sugarpaste icing you will have used to ice your cake)
- ♥ Rose petal cutters (available from sugarcraft shops)
- ♥ Dogbone tool (also available from sugarcraft shops)

1 Mix 25ml of cooled boiled water with a pea-sized amount of flower paste to form a glue.

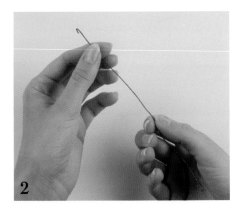

2 Bend a small hook in one end of a 24 gauge wire. Moisten with glue.

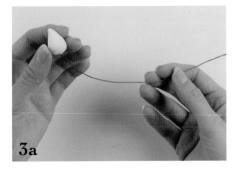

3a

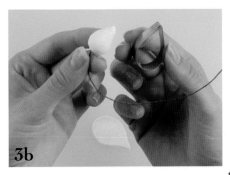

3b

3 Place a small piece of flower paste on the hooked wire and shape into a cone (a). The cone should be slightly smaller than the smallest petal cutter (b).

A clump of sugar roses

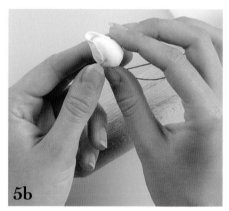

4 Roll out some flower paste as thinly as possible. Cut out one petal with your smallest cutter (a). Soften the edges using the dogbone tool (b).

5 Moisten the bottom of the petal with a little glue (a) and wrap around the cone (b). Put on one side to dry.

6 Make a second petal and wrap this around the first, leaving the top slightly open. If you study a real rose, you'll see what these inner petals should look like.

7 Cut out two more petals, and repeat the process, overlapping the edges.

8 Repeat step 7, but this time place three petals around the rose. Use your fingers to gently curl back the tops of these.

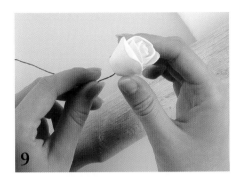

9 This time, use a petal cutter one size larger than your first cutter. Cut out four petals, soften the edges with the dogbone tool and make the centre of the petal slightly concave. Glue to your flower. You can curl back the tops of the petals using a cocktail stick if you wish.

10 You can stop here, or add another layer of petals. Make a variety of roses at various stages of openness to make them look as natural as possible.

A single sugar rose

The flowers can be made several months in advance, but you'll need to store them carefully. They should not be kept in a completely air-tight container – try piercing a few holes in the lid of a large plastic food container. Place a cushion or some wadding on the bottom, then put the flowers on top and then put some wadding over the top and place somewhere safe. This should be a reliable container in which to transport the flowers to your reception venue so they can be placed on your cake.

Use green flower paste to make leaves with which to enhance the sprays of roses

Adding your roses to your cake

You can make up whole sprays of roses, adding leaves cut out from green flower paste using leaf-shaped cutters or decorative gold leaves bought from sugarcraft shops. Secure the wires together using florist's tape to make sprays, then trail these down your cake, arranging them as naturally as possible.

Alternatively, if you only have time to make a few flowers, arrange them on a bed of tulle running round each layer of your cake. You could also use fake or real flowers for a similar look.

Hearts and Ribbons Cake

You will need:

♥ Small quantity of sugarpaste icing
♥ Colouring in your chosen colour
♥ Ribbon in a co-ordinating or contrasting colour
♥ Heart-shaped cutter
♥ Florist's wire

1 Colour your sugarpaste icing with your chosen colour. I prefer the specialist powder colours you can buy in cake decorating shops – conventional food colouring makes the icing sticky. Add a little colour at a time until you get the desired shade.

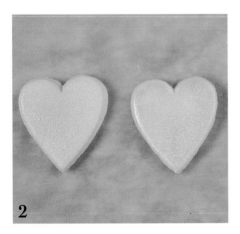

2

2 Roll out the icing until it is about 3 or 4mm thick. Using a heart-shaped cutter, cut out about 30 hearts. Place on greaseproof paper to dry. You could add some glitter at this stage for a glitzy finish!

3 Cut 30 lengths of 4¾in (12cm) each from the florist's wire. While the hearts are still soft, push a wire through the base of each until it is about two thirds of the way up the heart. Leave to dry overnight.

4 Assemble your tiers by stacking one directly on top of the other. Place ribbon around the base of each cake and secure each with a pin. (Don't forget to remove the pins before you cut the cake for your guests!)

5

5 Make a ribbon bow for the top of the cake. Secure using a pin. Make a second bow for the front – again use a pin to secure in place.

You can vary the design by doing hearts of different sizes or two different colours, or try a different shape such as stars or flowers. You don't have to use wires – you could place the flowers directly onto the cake itself using a little watered down sugar-paste as the glue.

79

6

6 Push the wired hearts into the cake, placing around four at the bottom tier bow, another three on the second tier and the majority at the top of the cake. You can bend the wire and manipulate the hearts until you get an arrangement that you like.

Silver-studded Cake

You will need:

♥ One ready-made bow
   from a stationery shop
♥ Silver balls (bought
   from any supermarket
   home-baking section)

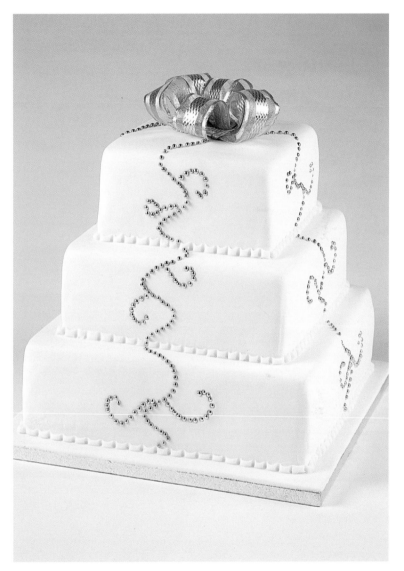

1 Choose your design. You could do a motif such as hearts or stars or go for a pattern such as the swirls on the cake above. Draw your design onto tracing paper.

2 Place your paper gently over your cake and using a pin, prick through onto the cake. Do it gently so that you can see the mark, but if you make a mistake you'll be able to smooth it away!

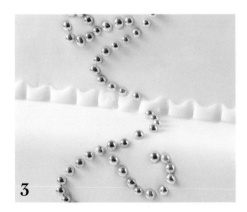

3

3 When you've pricked the design onto the cake, start adding the silver balls, pushing each one firmly into the icing

along the outline of the design. If they don't stick, try moistening them a little.

4 Finally, add the bow on top of the cake. You could of course put anything you want on top to complement your design.

Chocolate Wedding Cake

You will need:

♥ Two tiers (or more) of chocolate cake made from your favourite recipe. You could cheat and use a packet mix if you are short on time.
To ice each tier:
♥ 8¾oz (250gms) of dark chocolate

♥ 125 ml single cream
♥ 2 tsp glycerine
♥ 2 tsp golden syrup

If your tiers are very large, you might want to increase these quantities.

1 Cut the cakes so that each has a flat surface and stack.

2

If you have a chocolate wedding cake, you could save on the cost of dessert and serve the cake itself. Add lashings of double cream or Belgian chocolate ice-cream for a luxurious touch.

2 Put the icing ingredients in a heatproof bowl. Place the bowl in a large pan of simmering water and stir until melted.

3 Pour the melted chocolate icing over the cake and allow it to drip down the sides. Use a spatula to get an even covering. Place in a refrigerator for at least half an hour to set.

4 Decorate as you wish. You could use fresh strawberries if they are in season, red sugar roses, real flowers, red and gold ribbons or even chocolate truffles for that luxurious touch.

4

CHAPTER 7

The Photographs

However big or small your wedding, here's a few ideas for how to preserve those precious memories.

Start by deciding what style of photography you'd like for your wedding

This is one area where I'd advise caution before going DIY. Asking a friend or relative to take on the responsibility for your wedding photography is putting a lot of pressure on them. You might feel stressed about whether they will do a good enough job – but they will probably feel even more stressed!

Aside from the obvious financial advantage, there are other reasons to go DIY with your photos. If you want an informal wedding, you might feel more relaxed having your photographs taken by a friend. This way you can have as many photos taken as you like, keep every single print and get reprints whenever you want to, with no pressure to rush into ordering enlargements.

However, if you want something more artistic, such as the 'reportage-style' of wedding photography that has recently become popular, you would be better off with the experienced eye of a professional unless you have someone really talented in your family.

The traditional 'family groups' style is easier to take but remember your budding photographer doesn't just need to press the shutter, he or she will also have to organize everyone and get them in the right place.

Decide what photos you want, for example do you want some of the preparation before the wedding?

If this makes you decide to use a professional photographer, check what's included in the cost. Do you get a set of proofs? Also, check the cost of the reprints and whether you can spread the cost by ordering reprints over the course of a year or even two.

But if you still want to go DIY for your photographs, here are some practical and technical tips.

Practical tips

♥ Make a list of all the photos you want. Which family/group shots? Do you want photos of the bride getting ready? Do you want photos taken during the service? If so, what of? And does the church allow it?

There's a list of suggested photos at the end of this chapter, but of course, you can add to it or delete from it as you wish.

♥ You might also enlist a second person to help organize the guests for group photos. Give them a tick list so that they can make sure that you have every combination of friends and family that you want. Choose someone that knows most of your friends and family – your long lost cousin from Argentina might find the job a little difficult!

♥ Why not get two people to take the photos? Load one camera with black and white film and the other with colour. Colour photos will represent the day as you remember it. Black and white photos, however, are timeless. If you choose a reportage-style album of photos, then these should be done in black and white. Get the more skilful of your two photographers to take these!

♥ If you want more artistic shots, be specific about what you want. Again, it is a good idea to make a list. Collect images from wedding magazines and the internet showing the kind of look that you want and compile a scrapbook to pass on to your photographer.

Think about locations near your venue where you could recreate any pictures you particularly liked: stone steps, spiral staircases, old ruins, deserted beaches and old-fashioned swings can all look very artistic, especially in black and white.

However don't be tempted by locations too far from your venue.

♥ Go on a recce to where you plan to have your photos taken. Make a note of what will be in the background of the photos. Bear in mind that if you are using a public place, a passer-by could walk behind you and ruin your shot.

♥ An amateur photographer will probably find light conditions better in summer.

♥ Make sure you buy plenty of film. If you take ten rolls, 360 shots, you're bound to come away with some good ones! The film and developing will still add up to a fraction of the cost of a professional photographer.

♥ Put disposable cameras on each table as an additional back-up. But if you want the results to be worth the cost of developing, request that they are for adults to use only! Don't forget to ask someone to collect the cameras for you at the end of the reception and to look after them until you return from your honeymoon! If disposable cameras are out of your budget, just give each of your friends a film and let them take their own photos with their camera. You can still collect the films after and get them developed.

♥ If you are using a friend or family member as your photographer, don't forget to include them in some of the photos.

♥ Get the films developed at a professional lab. Though slightly more expensive, there'll be an appreciable difference in the quality of your prints and more opportunities to make adjustments to the finished image.

♥ Presentation makes all the difference. Invest time and money in choosing an album and think about how you want to mount and present your prints. Don't be afraid to resize your photos with the aid of a pair of scissors or, even better, a paper cutter.

♥ If you do end up disappointed by your photos, you can always get dressed up all over again and have a studio portrait taken – by a professional this time! Of course, this won't be the same as having a fantastic photo of the two of you on the day, but it's a good last resort!

Technical tips for the amateur photographer

♥ If you are using a 35mm camera, use a lens not less than 28mm for group shots since edge distortion will have people leaning at odd angles. Change this to an 85–105mm lens for head shots – this most closely resembles the human eye!

♥ If the bride or groom has a big nose, you could try using a 135mm lens for your head shots – this will compress perspective for a more flattering photo!

♥ Think about where the light will be when your photos are going to be taken. If the members of the bridal party are looking into the sun, they

Keep an eye out for original details to add to the overall atmosphere of your album

the light off a suitable white surface to avoid red-eye.

♥ Try to keep an eye out for small details. An intimate and tender look, nervous wringing of hands, gentle brushing away of hair from around the face or a tear dabbed from the eye can all add to the overall atmosphere that you can create in your wedding album.

♥ Finally, practise. Familiarize yourself with your camera well before the big day.

Suggested photos

The following list is just a suggestion. Use it, adapt it or make your own. However, don't go without a list altogether – be clear about which photos you would like to see in your wedding album.

If you or your groom has a large family, you might want to do several different combinations of family photograph. For example, bride and groom with bride's parents, bride and groom with their siblings, bride and groom with the bride's entire family including cousins, aunts and uncles and grandparents. If you want them to stand in a particular pecking order for this photo, make sure your photographer knows this or that they do!

If you have different groups of friends from different aspects of your life, you might want photos that reflect that. For example, bride and groom with the groom's colleagues, bride and groom with the

will squint. If the photographer is shooting into the sun, the bridal party's faces will be in shadow. Try and avoid either of these extremes.

♥ Shooting with the sun behind you can make the photo feel very flat whereas careful composition towards the sun will pick out lots of feature details. Don't be afraid to use your flashgun to provide the necessary fill-in to lighten the subjects' faces.

♥ Choice of flashgun is crucial. You'll need one with plenty of power and a high ISO rating. You'll also need to ensure that you have extra batteries immediately to hand. If you're going to use the flash for fill-in, make sure that it has a zoom attachment. However, if you're using the flash indoors, be sure to use a tilt and swivel flash so you can bounce

Before the ceremony

♥ Bride getting ready.

♥ Bridesmaids getting ready.

♥ Bride with the bridesmaids.

♥ Bride with her parents.

♥ Bride leaving for the ceremony.

♥ Groom getting ready.

♥ Groom waiting for the bride's arrival.

♥ Groom with the best man.

♥ Bride and her father arriving at the ceremony.

During the ceremony

♥ Bride walking up the aisle.

♥ Bride and groom at the altar.

♥ Exchanging rings.

♥ The first kiss.

♥ Signing the register.

♥ Walking back down the aisle together.

After the ceremony

♥ Bride and groom with bride's family.

♥ Bride and groom with groom's family.

♥ Bride and groom with both families.

♥ Bride and groom with bridesmaids, best man and ushers.

♥ Bride and bridesmaids.

♥ Groom, best man and ushers.

♥ Bride and groom with their closest friends.

♥ Bride and groom with all guests.

At the reception

♥ Bride and groom arriving at the reception.

♥ The receiving line.

♥ The cake table.

♥ The bridal table.

♥ The gift table.

♥ The bridal party seated at the bridal table.

♥ Cutting the cake.

♥ The first dance.

♥ The bride dancing with her father.

♥ The groom dancing with his mother-in-law.

♥ Throwing the bouquet.

♥ Bride and groom leaving the reception.

bride's old school friends. Thinking about this in advance will save time and hassle on the day and ensure that you manage to get all the photos that you want.

If your wedding is a true DIY wedding, and you've spent hours decorating your venue and doing your catering, you'll probably want extra photos to reflect your great achievement – the buffet table, the helium ballons, the cake, the menus, the seating plan and so on!

The video

These days, many people have digital camcorders and editing software is available quite cheaply for your PC, so a DIY video is definitely an option.

Anyone who has ever seen a home movie, however, will know that they just never look like the slick films that you see on your cinema and television screens. You will never achieve that with an amateur videographer and a home

camcorder, but there are things you can do to improve the results.

♥ The less movement the better. Obviously there are times when you want a close-up of the ceremony and times when you want a wide shot of the congregation, but in general, the camera should be kept still (use a tripod!) and the videographer's finger should resist using the zoom button too much! Get your videographer to frame his shot just before important moments and then leave the camera alone. He can then reframe for the next important moment. It's more important to have decent footage of the two of you exchanging your vows than it is to have Auntie Mabel singing 'All Things Bright and Beautiful'. During the less important moments of the ceremony the videographer can re-frame for his next shot.

♥ If you do zoom in, hold the shots immediately before and immediately after the zoom completely still for at least five seconds.

♥ Use two cameras. Set them up in different parts of the church, making sure that they don't end up filming each other! For the best results, write a plan of what you want each one to film and when, and schedule in time for each videographer to frame his/her shot. Don't schedule in for both cameras to be reframing at once or you won't have anything useable for your edited version. For example, camera 1 can be framing up for close-ups of your exchanging

of vows whilst camera 2 takes a wide shot of the congregation singing the preceding hymn. Both cameras should record the whole time, even when they are reframing. That way you can be sure of a continuous soundtrack. Keep your instructions simple however and sit down with both videographers together to make sure they understand the plan. Once again, whenever possible get your videographers to keep their cameras still and not zoom in and out too much!

♥ Think about the logistics: is there anywhere to plug in and get mains power to each camera? Will one tape be long enough to record the whole ceremony? If you're using two cameras, you might want to organize them so that they don't change tapes and/or batteries at the same time!

♥ If you don't have a good camcorder, hire one!

♥ Sound is one of the biggest problems in amateur videos. Hire a good microphone with a long lead to plug into your camera. Place it on a microphone stand as close as possible to where the vows will be exchanged. Check that the vicar or registrar is happy with this. Before the wedding, put new long-life batteries into the microphone.

If you zoom in, hold the shots immediately before and after the zoom for at least five seconds

93

CHAPTER 8

The Flowers

From the bouquet that you carry, to the arrangement on your buffet table, the right flowers can add a real touch of luxury to your big day.

Doing your own flowers can work out cheaper, but you need to consider the amount of work involved. Bouquets should be made the day before your wedding at the earliest if you want them to look their best, so think about how many other jobs you will have during the week leading up to the wedding and how many helpers you will have. It would be difficult, though not impossible, to do both your own flowers and your own catering.

If you just want to do your own flowers in order to save money, you should calculate all the costs carefully in advance before making the decision to go ahead. Factor in the cost of buying not only the flowers for the day itself but also flowers and foliage for practising beforehand plus the tools you will

need: green floral tape, florists wire, bouquet holders, wired ribbon, secateurs, wire cutters and plenty of containers.

Buying lots of flowers can get very expensive. You might want to visit a flower market the day before the wedding or see if you can come to an arrangement with a local florist or market stall if you are buying in bulk.

If you have no previous experience of floristry, you might wish to attend evening classes. Include the fees for that in your budget.

Draw up a list of the flowers you'll need: buttonholes for the groom, best man, ushers and both fathers and corsages for both the bride's and the groom's mother. Traditionally, the groom's buttonhole should be made up from the same flowers as the bride's bouquet and might be a different colour from the others to distinguish him from the rest of the group.

Prepare your flowers carefully. When you get the blooms home, cut about ¾in (2cm) off the bottom of each stem. It's best to cut on a diagonal to increase the surface area for the flower to take up water. Take off thorns and any leaves that are below half way down the stem. Put the flowers in a large bucket of tepid water and add some flower food. They should rest there for about 6–12 hours before you start working with them. Change the water at least once a day.

Money-saving alternatives to arranging your own flowers

♥ Find out if anyone else is getting married at the same church as you on the same day. You might be able to share the cost of the decorations – as long as your tastes coincide.

♥ Buy a ready-made bouquet from a local florist: choose one that is already made up and order the same thing – at the same price – for you and your bridesmaids, making sure they leave off the polythene! You might finish the bouquet off with a ribbon to match your bridesmaids' dresses or ask the florist to do this for you. Remember to organize someone to pick these bouquets up on the big day.

♥ Simple is often stylish. Consider carrying just one exotic bloom such as a cala lily. If you're tall and slim and wearing a long fitted dress, this could be just the thing!

♥ Consider buying the more important flowers like your bouquet and an arrangement for the church, and then doing the remainder yourself, such as buttonholes and table decorations.

♥ Instead of expensive floral table decorations, look for ready-made table centres. Choose something that you can re-use at future events such as striking candlesticks or bowls of floating candles. If you end up with too many, you could always give some as presents or sell them off at a car boot sale.

♥ If you are using a florist, choose a bouquet with lots of greenery – this will be cheaper!

♥ Choosing blooms that are in season can also significantly reduce the costs.

Buttonhole

For each buttonhole you will need:

- ♥ 1 rose
- ♥ 5 rose leaves
- ♥ Gutta-percha tape
- ♥ Heavy gauge stub wire
- ♥ Silver rose wire

1 The first thing you need to do is wire your rose leaves. Take a single leaf and a length of rose wire. Thread the wire through the main vein at the back of the leaf about two thirds of the way up.

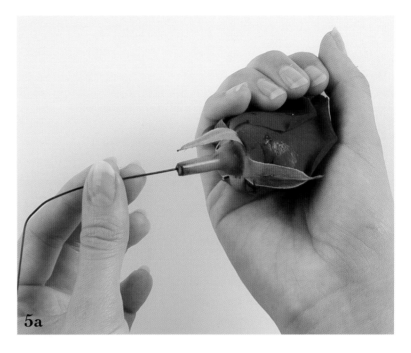

2 Very gently bring the ends of the wire back down towards the stem and twist one around the stem and the other end.

3 Repeat this with the other leaves, but just go as far as Step 1 with the fifth leaf.

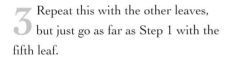

4 Make a three-leafed sprig using two of the finished leaves and the fifth leaf. Place the three leaves together with the fifth leaf on the right-hand side. Then twist the wires of this leaf around all three stems so that the leaves are joined together.

5 Now wire the rose. Cut the stem about ⅔in (1.5cm) below the calyx. Push the stub wire up the stem and into the seed box (a). Then push a rose wire through the flower head at its base (b).

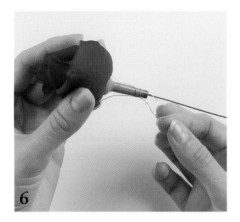

6 Gently bring the ends of the rose wire down and wrap one of the ends around the other one and the stub wire, binding them together. Tape down the wires from the top of the stem.

7 Place the wired rose on top of the three-leafed sprig and tape together.

8 Finish off by taping the two single leaves underneath the flower. Gently bend the wires so that the leaves sit neatly in place.

Why not use roses from your garden for your bouquet and buttonhole? Then you'll have a reminder of your special day year after year. If you don't have any plan ahead and plant some specially, but be sure to choose a variety that blooms at the time of your wedding!

Corsage

**For each corsage
you will need:**

♥ 1 small lily head
♥ 2 lily buds
♥ Wax flowers
♥ Bear grass
♥ Gutta-percha tape
♥ Heavy gauge stub wire
♥ Silver rose wire

1 Using silver rose wire, wire your lily flower as described for the rose in the previous project. Leave the buds on their stems, but push a length of wire through each bud and bring down on each side of the stem. Tape all the wires.

2 Arrange two pieces of bear grass with the two lily buds on the left. Balance the buds by placing a few wax flower stems on the right of the bear grass. When you are satisfied with how your arrangement is looking, bind it together securely using florists' tape.

3 Complete the corsage by adding the open lily just above where you have taped the other stems together. Bind the flower in place. Complete by bringing one or two stems of bear grass over the top of the flower and taping in place.

Hand-tied Bridal Bouquet

You will need:

- ♥ 3 stems of lilies, with a mixture of buds and flowers on each
- ♥ 6 roses in a complementary or contrasting colour
- ♥ Gypsophila or wax flowers
- ♥ Bear grass
- ♥ Eucalyptus
- ♥ Twine
- ♥ Scissors
- ♥ Secateurs
- ♥ Ribbon to finish off

2 The stems are going to be built up in a spiral as this will make the bunch easy for you to hold. Start with a small bunch of eucalyptus. Take a long piece of twine and bind these together.

1 Choose your flowers carefully. Discard any that are blemished. Remove the thorns from the roses and the lower leaves from the stems. Clean the stems if necessary – the last thing you want is dirt on your dress! Remove any powdery stamens from the lilies too or you could end up with a nasty stain.

3 Take one of your three lily stems. Lay one on top of the eucalyptus vertically. Then take two stems of

gypsophila or wax flowers. Place the first on a diagonal going from left to right. Holding the bouquet with your left hand, use your right hand to place the other stem of gypsophila behind the bouquet so that it goes from right to left. Bind with twine to hold firmly in place.

4 Keep adding a mixture of foliage and flowers, always placing a stem across the front of the bouquet diagonally from left to right and then a stem at the back from right to left.

5 Bind stems a few at a time as this will make it easier for you to handle and means that if you make a mistake, you can go back a few steps instead of starting over again.

6 Aim at building up a dome shape. Keep rotating the bouquet and viewing it from different angles to ensure it looks good all the way round. You might find it easier to work with a friend or keep a large vase handy so you can stand the bouquet up and view your work in progress.

7

7 When you are happy with your results, tie the twine off in a knot. Then trim the stems to make the base of the bouquet flat so you can stand it in a vase until your wedding.

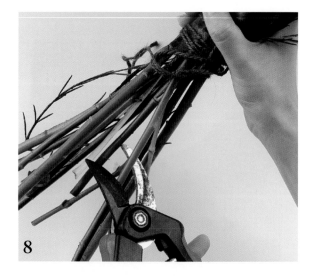

8

8 Finish the bouquet off with a ribbon and stand in a vase in a cool place.

Cut Flower Table Centrepiece

You can adapt this centrepiece to suit your colour scheme, or to make use of the flowers in your garden or whatever blooms are available cheaply in your local shops.

For each centrepiece, you will need:

♥ A tray
♥ An oasis (use 'wet' rather than 'dry' oasis)
♥ Candle and candle holder

♥ Flowers and foliage, e.g. carnations, roses, lilies, gypsophila, bear grass, eucalyptus

1 Cut your oasis to a suitable size to fit your tray then soak it thoroughly.

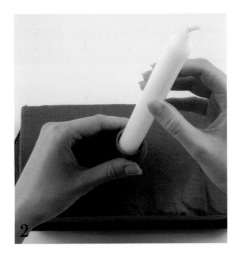

2 Insert a candle holder into the oasis and put the candle in place. You can use more than one candle if you prefer.

3 Work around the sides of the oasis adding a few short sprigs of foliage to gradually build up the arrangement.

4 Begin to add your main flowers to the arrangement. Remember this is a table centre so it will be seen from all sides. You therefore need to ensure that the flowers are dispersed evenly throughout the arrangement.

5 Work around the arrangement, adding smaller flowers and foliage to cover the oasis entirely. You should be aiming for soft edges.

Table Centrepiece Using Plants

For each centrepiece, you will need:

- ♥ A suitable waterproof container
- ♥ Compost
- ♥ Candle and candle holder (optional)
- ♥ A selection of potted plants in co-ordinating colours, such as miniature roses, heathers and pansies
- ♥ Clay balls
- ♥ Broken terracotta pieces (if using a flower pot)

The advantage of using pot plants from a garden centre rather than cut flowers is that the arrangements can be made in advance. If you're confident with houseplants, you could make these up to two weeks before the actual wedding day.

Again, adapt this centrepiece to suit your colour scheme and to suit the season. For example, rather than using pot plants, you could grow hyacinths or daffodils in pots for a spring wedding. You'll need to plant these in the autumn. There is a risk element here of course – they might bloom too early or too late or not at all – so have a contingency plan!

Choose the colour of your pot carefully. If you want that ultra-co-ordinated look, take a petal from your plant to your local DIY store and get them to match the shade of paint to the petal.

Painted terracotta pots can go mouldy when they get wet, and obviously you will need to water your arrangement. You could either coat your pot in watered down PVA glue before painting or you could pot your plants in a plastic pot and place this inside your painted terracotta pot on the morning of the wedding.

1 Place the clay balls in the bottom of the container, on top of the terracotta pieces if you are using them. This ensures good drainage.

2 Half fill the pot with compost. If it is a hot summer, and you're a bit forgetful about watering, you can buy a special gel to mix with your compost that will mean you don't have to water quite so often!

108

3

Tap the plants gently and remove them from their pots. Place in the pot and rearrange until you get a combination that you are happy with. In general, put the taller plants in the centre and the smaller ones around the edge. The plants should be quite close together so that you can't see any soil.

Add compost in between the plants until the pot is full. If there is soil visible, you can place some coloured stones or glass beads over the top to conceal it.

CHAPTER 9

The Dress

How to save money without

compromising how you look!

The image that is perhaps most associated with weddings is that of a bride in an extravagant white dress. Perhaps you've been dreaming since of that day when you walk down the aisle in your dream wedding dress and, if so, far be it from me to suggest you shouldn't go to town and spend a fortune! However, there are many brides out there who want to look fantastic on their wedding day, but either don't have much money to spend on their dress or simply don't want to spend a great deal on a garment they will only wear once. So what are the alternatives?

Making your own dress

If you are a competent seamstress and can find a pattern and fabric that you like, great!

If you've never stitched a garment in your life, your own wedding dress probably isn't the easiest place to start! If you are still determined to have a go, it might be a good idea to try going to an evening dressmaking class or at least to try making a simpler garment such as a skirt to be sure that it is something that you really want to pursue. Even something that looks easy, such as sewing a straight seam, requires skill, so get some leftover pieces of fabric and get practising!

But before you plunge in and make the dress itself, make sure you know what sort of dress will suit you. The advantage of buying a dress in a shop is that you can try it on first and check that you look good. That slinky, silky dress that looked great on the model in the bridal magazine might not work so well on you. Even if you are making your own dress, unless you are absolutely sure about what will suit you and what won't, go to a few shops and try some dresses on.

Once you've got an idea of the shape and style you like, go ahead and look for a pattern. Don't forget to consider colour when you are

The image most associated with weddings is that of the bride in her classic white dress

choosing – whether you are making your own dress or buying one! Most brides imagine themselves in a traditional white dress, but white is not the easiest colour to wear and simply does not suit everybody. You might be better with ivory, cream or even a subtle shade of blue!

Take a trusted friend with you and try on a few dresses in different shades at a bridal shop. You could also ask the assistant's advice – getting this advice does not oblige you to purchase the garment.

If you sew your own clothes a lot, you'll know which pattern manufacturers make patterns that are a good fit for you and which ones don't. If you don't, it's going to be trial and error. Bridal fabrics can be very expensive, and you can't afford to make any mistakes. It is a good idea to practise first using cheaper fabric to make sure you get the right style and fit before cutting into that expensive silk! However, bear in mind that a dress cut in a cheap lightweight fabric will not hang in the way that the same dress made out of rich and heavy brocade does. Look for fabric at end-of-season clearance sales. Alternatively, you can buy beautiful fabrics, often at very reasonable prices, from ethnic shops.

A simple style is obviously going to be easier to make than an elaborate one. Going for a simple style and decorating the dress with lace and beading will be easier.

Handling the vast lengths of fabric that you will need for a very full wedding dress is difficult at the best of times, but if you are working in a confined space it is going to be virtually impossible. Consider the practicalities of making the dress. Is there a room you can set aside for this? If you are going to lay your fabric out on the floor to cut out the pieces, make sure you vacuum thoroughly, especially if you have pets!

A simple style is going to be easier to make than an elaborate one

Alternatives to DIY

If you can't sew, you can still get a great wedding dress without spending a fortune.

♥ *Find a pattern and material that you like, and approach a dressmaker to make it for you. But cost out the materials and the cost of the dressmaker carefully before you commit yourself – you may find it more expensive than buying a dress at a conventional wedding shop!*

♥ *Why not go for a white or pale-coloured evening gown? You could end up with that designer label that you've always wanted in your wardrobe for the cost of the average wedding dress, plus you'll be able to wear it again. If you don't want to wear something white again you could have it professionally dyed after the wedding. Wearing the dress again has an added advantage – it helps keep you the same size as you were on your wedding day!*

♥ *Buy your dress second-hand or vintage. Try charity shops and vintage clothes shops, the classifieds or an advertisement on a wedding website. Some shops specialize in dresses that have been worn once – try looking in your local telephone directory. You might even find that your mum, aunt or grandma has a dress you can borrow for the day.*

♥ *Even if you don't want to wear second-hand on your big day, somebody else will! Sell your dress afterwards. You'll always have the photos for your memories!*

♥ *Plan ahead and buy your dress in the sales. However, be careful if your weight is prone to fluctuate or if you are planning a diet before the big day. If necessary, you can always get a dressmaker to make a few last-minute alterations, but if you've put on ten pounds this could be difficult!*

♥ *Buy your dress, shoes, underwear and veil in the same shop and try to negotiate a discount.*

♥ *Opt for a simple dress and go for stylish, eye-catching accessories.*

Accessories

Gone are the days when the only place you could buy the requisite white lacy underwear, white silk sandals and tiaras was the bridal shop. Now you have more choice at more competitive prices.

Bridal underwear is easy to find on the high street. Choose something that you will wear again, but make sure you try it on under your dress!

High street stores also sell white, ivory and pale pastel-coloured shoes and sandals. If you are having a winter wedding, you might find it easier to get these if you buy them in the summer before your wedding. You shouldn't, however, buy the shoes until after you have bought the dress.

If you can't find what you are looking for on the high street, try the classifieds or advertisements on wedding internet sites. Wedding shoes have usually only been worn once, so you're quite likely to pick up a bargain in good condition.

You can always buy plain shoes and dress these up with sequins or other trimmings. Many department stores and craft shops sell ready-made decorations that would be suitable for this.

If you aren't used to high heels, it's a mistake to buy these for your wedding day, unless you're going to practise a lot beforehand. You will spend a long time standing up on your wedding day and the last thing you want is sore feet!

Don't wear high heels on your wedding day unless you are very used to them, as opportunities to rest your feet may be few and far between!

115

Making a Simple Veil

The instructions below will give you a veil that is moderately full, hanging to just below your shoulders in front of your face and to your hips behind. Either adapt the instructions if you want a different length or buy a pattern for the size and degree of fullness that you want.

You will need:

- ♥ Rectangle of white, cream or ivory tulle approximately 63in (160cm) wide and 6½ft (2m) long
- ♥ Sewing machine
- ♥ Scissors
- ♥ Thread
- ♥ Clear plastic comb
- ♥ Sequins and pearls (optional)

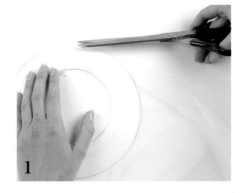

1

1 Using a plate or a saucer as a guide, cut the corners of the rectangle off so that they are round.

2

2 Using a sewing machine set on a shallow zig-zag stitch, sew around the edge of the veil. You can use matching thread or a contrasting colour.

3 Decorate the edges of your veil using pearls and sequins if you wish. For most of your wedding, the front portion of your veil – the first 27½in (70cm) – will be behind you so you need to sew the decorations on the wrong side for this section.

4 Hand stitch across the veil 27½in (70cm) from the top using running stitch then gather the material.

5 Still using your needle and thread, attach the veil to the comb, making a stitch around each tooth.

CHAPTER 10

The Jewellery

Start threading those beads!

Here's some ideas for

inexpensive jewellery to

compliment your outfit.

W edding jewellery falls into two distinct categories. The most important items are your rings and it is vital to think carefully before economizing here as you will be wearing them for the rest of your lives. The second category of wedding jewellery is that which you will wear on your big day to complement your dress. If you're on a budget, there is no need to spend a fortune here. You can buy beautiful pieces of costume jewellery on the high street, borrow something from a friend or you might even consider making your own – some ideas are provided at the end of this chapter.

Wedding jewellery falls into two main categories; the rings and that which you will wear on the day to complement your dress

The rings

The most important thing to consider when choosing your wedding and engagement rings is that they need they need to have lasting appeal. Obviously you must be careful to stay within budget but do remember that, apart from the marriage itself, this is the most lasting item from your wedding day so it does make sense to allocate a substantial part of your budget to it and purchase something you are both really happy with.

Once you have set a budget for rings, try to focus only within that budget when you visit the jewellers. Don't let yourself be tempted into trying on rings you can't afford – it will only seduce you into spending too much or make you feel dissatisfied with what you can afford to buy.

An informed decision is always better than one made in ignorance. Discuss the various merits of white gold versus platinum with your jeweller and look at friends' rings to see how much the metal has discoloured or lost its shine. If you are choosing a diamond engagement ring, bear in mind that diamonds are not just valued on their size but also on the amount of impurity and imperfections within the stone. Ask about the quality of the stone you are buying and compare prices around several jewellers.

Choose rings that suit your lifestyle. If you play a lot of sport, choose a ring that will be suitable to

wear during this activity. If you need to keep removing it, you will risk losing it.

Use a soft toothbrush and warm water with a little washing-up liquid to keep your engagement ring clean, you do not need to buy specialist jewellery cleaner. Have your engagement ring cleaned professionally by a jeweller just before your wedding so that it looks sparkly on the photos!

It is vital to think carefully before economizing on your wedding rings as you will be wearing them for the rest of your life

Making a Tiara

You will need:

- ♥ A tiara base in silver or gold
- ♥ Beads of your choice
- ♥ Silver or gold

- jewellery wire to match your base
- ♥ Small pliers
- ♥ Wire cutters

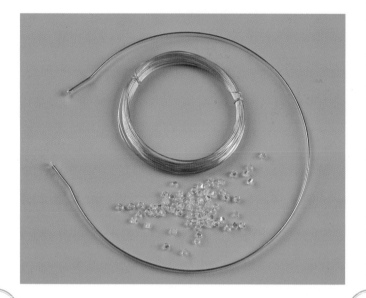

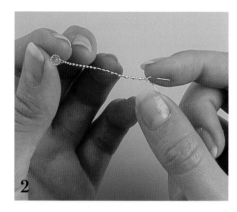

2 Starting from the bead, twist the ends of the wire together repeatedly until you reach the bottom of the wire to make an 'antenna'.

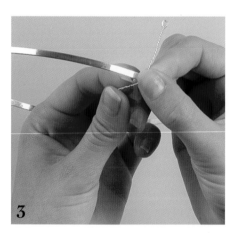

3 Hold the antenna in front of the tiara base in the centre. Twist the wire underneath the base, bringing it behind, over the top and back underneath the base.

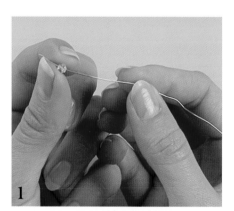

1 Cut a length of wire about 4¾in (12cm) long. Thread a bead onto this wire so that the bead is in the middle.

one height or vary the heights as you prefer. Leave a few centimetres empty at each end of the base to slide into your hair.

4 Continue making antennae and adding them to the tiara, working from the centre outwards. Make them all

5 When you are happy with the number and positioning of antennae, take a long length of wire and twist it around the base, working from one end to the other. This neatens the ends of the antennae.

Making Earrings

You will need:

- ♥ Pair of fishhooks in silver or gold (you will find these in bead and craft shops)
- ♥ Pair of headpins in silver or gold
- ♥ Beads of your choice
- ♥ Small pliers
- ♥ Wire cutters

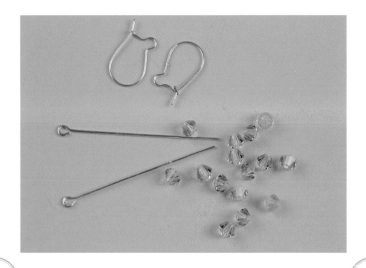

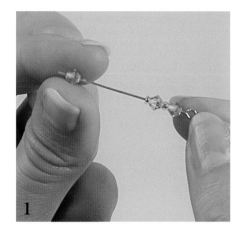

1 Thread the beads of your choice onto the headpin. You can space these out with a smaller bead between each if you want to.

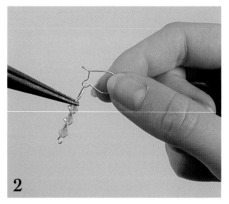

2 Place the top of the headpin through the hoop on the fishhook and twist to secure.

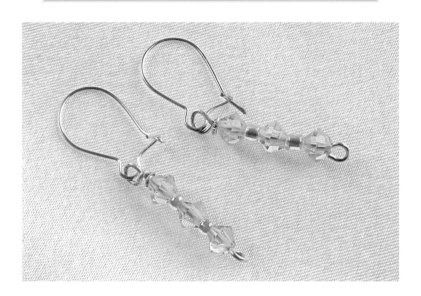

Making a Necklace

You will need:

♥ A three-row clasp in silver or gold
♥ Beads of your choice
♥ Clear plastic thread or thin silver or gold jewellery wire if you prefer
♥ Clear nail varnish

2 Thread beads onto the plastic thread to within ¾in (2cm) of the loose end. Again, you can intersperse the larger beads with smaller ones if preferred.

3 Pull the loose end through the top hoop on the other side of the clasp so that the beads come all the way up to the clasp. Tie it off with a knot and secure with clear nail varnish.

4 Repeat steps 1–3 twice, using a thread of 21in (54cm) for the middle loop and 23in (58cm) for the bottom loop.

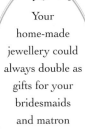

Your home-made jewellery could always double as gifts for your bridesmaids and matron of honour.

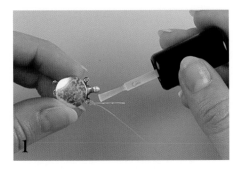

1 Take a length of plastic thread 19½in (50cm) long. Tie this in a knot through the top hoop on one side of the clasp. Dab with clear nail varnish – this stops the knot from undoing itself.

CHAPTER 11

The Reception Venue

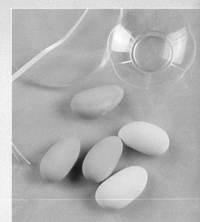

How to achieve that five-star

look on a two-star budget!

For the average wedding, hiring the venue for the reception will take up quite a large proportion of the budget. With money to spend, and enough notice, you can easily find somewhere that will be the perfect setting to celebrate your marriage. But what about if you're on a tight budget?

If you're on a budget, you might be able to get a discount if you book a long way in advance. Alternatively, you could hold your wedding on a weekday – because this is a less popular option it is often possible to negotiate a good price. However, it will pose more of a problem with attendance if your wedding is on a weekday. Weigh up the options carefully: saving money on that venue that you really want versus having all your nearest and dearest there to witness your big day.

Hiring a venue

Compile a list of questions relevant to your reception, and take the list with you when you meet with the manager of any possible venues. Here are some suggestions:

♥ What's included – Flowers? Welcome drinks? Entertainment?
♥ Will it cost extra to have an evening party as well?
♥ Do they provide caterers or do you need to organize that?
♥ Can you choose to do your own catering and flowers if you want to or will they insist on using their own suppliers?

♥ Do they charge for corkage if you supply your own drinks?
♥ What colour table linen is available?
♥ If the venue is a hotel, will preferential room rates be offered to your guests?
♥ Is there a cake stand you can use and an easel for displaying your seating plan?
♥ Is there ample parking?
♥ How long will it take to travel there from your church or registry office?
♥ How child-friendly is it?
♥ Is there plenty of access for disabled guests?

If you are having a civil ceremony, you might be able to find a venue where you can hold both the ceremony and the reception. This might save on venue costs and you'll spend less on transport too!

Hire a marquee. If you're having caterers, you might also be able to hire a marquee through them. If not, try a specialist firm who will be able to advise you on how large a venue will be adequate for your needs. Look at photographs of your chosen marquee or, even better, see it erected. Find out what's included – you might have to pay extra for a service marquee for caterers, toilets, dance floor, heating and delivery.

If these options still prove too expensive, don't despair. Here are some more cost-effective ideas for places to hold your reception:

♥ If you're getting married in a church, why not have your wedding in the church hall? You'll save money if you don't need to transport to the reception. Even a drab church hall will look better by candlelight so hold your wedding later in the day. Fill the hall with flowers and swags of tulle or voile and no-one will notice the colour of the walls! Even better, spend some of the money you are saving on brightly coloured helium balloons: you can buy them ready-filled or buy a canister of gas and fill them yourselves. It doesn't cost much more to get a professional in to put a balloon arch over your buffet table and balloon bouquets on all the guest tables and the end results will be well worth it!

♥ If you're an optimist, brave the weather and have an enormous picnic in the park, by a river or even on a beach! Take gazebos just in case (you can buy large gazebos very cheaply at DIY stores) and ask your guests to bring deck chairs and picnic rugs.

♥ Hire a room at a pub. Some pubs will refund your hire costs if your guests spend enough at the bar! Check you'll be allowed to bring your own food or you could get a traditional pub meal served instead.

If you are having a civil ceremony, you might be able to hold the ceremony and the reception in the same place

Why not decorate your venue with some enlarged photographs of you and your fiancé when you were children? It will certainly entertain your guests!

If you are holding your reception in a hired room or a church hall, you will need time to decorate it yourself. Bear in mind that this might bring extra costs, for example you might need to pay for the hire a day or even two days beforehand. Allow some money in your budget for decorations as you will find that candles, balloons, tablecloths and so on will soon add up.

Decorating your venue on a budget

♥ Buy lengths of fabric such as organza to use instead of tablecloths, or as runners, to add a touch of glamour. If you're supplying your own table linen, sew or pin swags of brightly coloured voile round the edge of each table. This will use less fabric than making a real swagged table cloth and it will look just as good.

♥ Buy rolls of lining paper from a DIY store or plain paper tablecloths from a supermarket and use these as your tablecloths. Place some coloured crayons on each table and let your guests do the decorating. It will keep the children present quiet during the speeches and you might end up with some nice souvenirs of your day.

♥ Use tealights as place markers – print each guest's name on a piece of paper and glue it around the base.

♥ Scatter table confetti, shells, rose petals or even colourful sweets on the tables.

♥ A fireworks display could transform the dullest of venues. You can buy a DIY wedding display or alternatively you might feel safer getting a professional operator to run the display for you – that way you'll be covered by public liability insurance too. You can also check your local telephone directory for suppliers.

♥ For simple table centres, get individual wedding cakes made for each table. This would be very cost-effective combining not only your cake and your centrepiece but the cakes could be your favours or even dessert!

♥ Helium-filled balloons make an effective and inexpensive table centre. You could weight them down using a glass bowl filled with glass beads or, for an even cheaper option, place a balloon filled with water into a small wedding cake box to act as the weight.

♥ A bowl of fruit could be placed on each table as a cheap and easy table centre. It has the added advantage of being an extra dessert too!

♥ A glass bowl filled with water and floating candles would make a pretty and inexpensive table centre. Scatter a few rose petals on the water too and around the bowl on the table. You can always give the bowls away afterwards as presents to those people who helped with your wedding.

♥ Don't forget that there are two easy floral table centres for you to make in Chapter 8!

Wedding Favours

For each favour you will need:

♥ At least 2 circles of tulle or sheer fabric
♥ Ribbon to tie
♥ 3 or 4 sugared almonds
♥ A small plastic cup

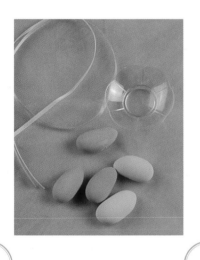

Traditional favours are made of voile and ribbons placed in a glass bowl. To make them more elaborate use more circles of fabric, perhaps in two contrasting colours, and extra ribbons or, if you used silk flowers on your stationery, continue the theme and add one or two when you tie the ribbon.

2 Gather the circles together around the cup and tie with a ribbon. Insert a flower at this point if you wish.

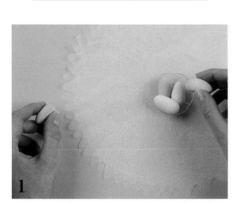

1 Lay the circles on top of each other, place the plastic cup in the centre and the almonds inside the cup.

131

CHAPTER 12

Transport, Entertainment and Honeymoon

How to get there, how to make your reception go with a swing and what to do to recuperate afterwards... all on a budget of course!

Transport

Many limousine and chauffeur companies charge more for a wedding than for other events. So what can you do to avoid paying through the nose for transport on your wedding day?

♥ Ring and get a quote for an ordinary event first. When you phone back and ask for a quote for your wedding, if it's higher, ask why!

♥ Think of an alternative to traditional wedding cars: do you have a friend with a high-class,

If you have a friend with a characterful means of transport, ask them to be your chauffeur for the day

vintage or characterful car who would agree to be your chaffuer?

♥ If you want to arrive in style, but don't want to spend a fortune for a few minutes travel, why not hire a classic car for a few days? Get a friend to drive you to the wedding in it, then drive off into the sunset for a memorable start to your honeymoon! It might be expensive – probably more than a conventional wedding car, but you'll have several days' rather than a few minutes of enjoyment!

♥ If you live near the church, do two trips using just one car. Your bridesmaids should go first and then the car should return for you and your father.

♥ Choose a reception venue near enough to the church or registry office to walk to so that you can just hire the cars for the short time before your wedding. Have a contingency plan in case of bad weather – no bride wants to arrive looking like a drowned rat.

To get better value for money from a hire car, use it again at the end of the day to drive off into the sunset for your honeymoon!

Entertainment

♥ Don't book too much entertainment. Photographs, dinner and speeches always take longer than you think and you should allow plenty of time to talk to your guests. Opt for a live band or a disco rather than both.

♥ Again, bands and DJs sometimes charge more for a wedding than an ordinary party. Getting a quote for a party first will ensure you know your DJ's normal rate and stop you from getting ripped off.

♥ Make compilation tapes or CDs of your favourite songs. Check them thoroughly for mistakes and make sure you have recorded enough material for the entire evening. You might want to ask an outgoing friend to act as DJ!

♥ A giant 'Jenga' game or a giant chess set could keep both adults and children entertained.

♥ Hold a barn dance or buy a karaoke machine (these are available quite cheaply on the high street) for an alternative to the usual entertainment.

♥ Provide coloured pencils, plenty of paper and toys for your younger guests. Colouring books and dot-to-dots can be found cheaply in bargain stores.

♥ There's no rule that says you have to have entertainment. If you'd rather just have a short reception where you eat a meal and talk to your guests, do that. Make it clear on your invitations that that is what will be on offer so that no-one comes along expecting a big knees-up and ends up going away disappointed!

Honeymoon

The same rules apply to honeymoons as to any holiday if you want to bag a bargain.

♥ Booking your flights and accommodation separately might work out cheaper. Our two weeks in the jungle in Costa Rica would have cost double if we had gone on a package deal. But this isn't always the case so check carefully.

♥ If you haven't got your heart set on a particular destination, you could wait and try to get a late bargain.

♥ Ask for honeymoon vouchers as your wedding present for the holiday of a lifetime. Remember, don't have to have your honeymoon immediately after your wedding.

♥ Going on an all-inclusive package will give you the advantage of knowing how much you're spending.

♥ Many people find it's much cheaper to get married abroad. Take advantage of free wedding packages offered at some destinations. You could end up with a free wedding cake or flowers.

♥ Use the internet. There are many websites at which you can book four- and five-star hotels at discount prices: www.expedia.com, www.laterooms.com and www.ratestogo.com are all good ones to try. Similarly, you can find bargain flights and even book your hire-car online.

♥ Look at the current exchange rates to find out which destinations offer the best value for money.

Many people find it cheaper to get married abroad

135

Useful Addresses

General wedding websites

www.diybrides.co.uk
Jenny Hopkin's website designed especially to accompany this book, with more hints, tips and ideas plus the chance to see your DIY wedding featured on the website, or to read the personal success stories of other DIY brides.

www.wedding-service.co.uk
Useful directory of wedding services across the UK.

www.weddingguide.co.uk
The UK's first wedding website, with useful forums and chatrooms where you can exchange information with other brides (and grooms) and useful articles to help you plan every aspect of your wedding.

www.confetti.co.uk
A great source of information, this site features the usual message boards and articles, but you can also shop online. At the time of going to press, confetti also has two shops in the UK, in London and in Leeds.

www.hitched.co.uk
Full of useful information, with everything from waxed seals to a countdown clock to buy online.

www.bridesave.com
American website with lots of hints and tips that are equally useful for UK brides.

www.ezweddingplanner.com
Free software to help you plan all aspects of your wedding

www.the-wedding-planner.com
American website providing a useful list of wedding businesses.

Craft supplies
– stationery
Craft Creations Limited
Ingersoll House
Delamare Road
Cheshunt
Hertfordshire
EN8 9HD, United Kingdom
Tel: 0044 (0)1992 781900
www.craftcreations.co.uk
Good mail order service available.

HobbyCraft Group Limited
7 Enterprise Way
Aviation Park
Bournemouth International
Airport
Christchurch
Dorset
BH23 6HG, United Kingdom
Tel: 0044 (0)1202 596100
www.hobbycraft.co.uk
*A range of stores across the UK
stocking a wide variety of craft
supplies.*

Mad about Cards
42 North Street
Great Wakering
Southend-on-Sea
Essex SS3 0EL
United Kingdom
www.madaboutcards.co.uk
*Offers excellent online ordering
service.*

Wrap With Us
277 Robbins Lane
Syosset
NY 11791
Tel: 011 1(516) 942 7890 /
011 1(800) 962 0891
www.wrapwithus.com
*Quality wedding favours,
personalized ribbons and
invitations at low pirces with
volume discounts available.*

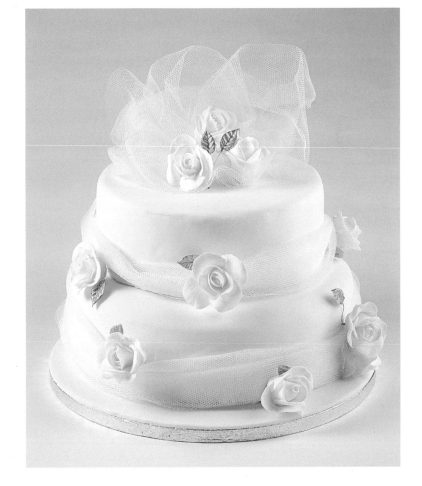

Craft supplies – Cake

Sugarshack

Suppliers of all your cake decorating needs including sugarpaste icing.

87 Burntoak Broadway

Burntoak, Middx HA8 5EP

FREEPHONE: 0800 597 5097

(UK Only) INTERNATIONAL:

+44 (0)20 8952 4260

FAX: +44 (0)20 8951 4888

www.sugarshack.co.uk

Flowers

www.flowers.org.uk

The website of the Flowers and Plants Association. Good source of general information about flowers, plus specific ideas for weddings.

Dress

www.1stcallforweddings.co.uk

1st Call for Weddings stocks second hand dresses from top designers. On this site, you can buy and sell wedding gowns, bridesmaids dresses and mother of the bride outfits.

Jewellery

Creative Beadcraft

Unit 2

Asheridge Business Centre

Asheridge Road

Chesham

Buckinghamshire

HP5 2PT, United Kingdom

Tel: 0044 (0)1494 778818

http://www.creativebeadcraft.co.uk/

For jewellery findings and beads, which can be ordered online or visit their shop at 20, Beak Street, London W1.

Honeymoons

www.lastminute.com

For last minute holiday bargains.

www.teletextholidays.co.uk

For last minute holiday bargains.

www.laterooms.com

Find hotel rooms at discount prices across the world.

www.ratestogo.com

Another website with great hotel prices.

Index

PHOTOGRAPHY

ART TECHNIQUES

VIDEOS

MAGAZINES

WOODTURNING • WOODCARVING
FURNITURE & CABINETMAKING
THE ROUTER • NEW WOODWORKING
THE DOLLS' HOUSE MAGAZINE
OUTDOOR PHOTOGRAPHY
BLACK & WHITE PHOTOGRAPHY
TRAVEL PHOTOGRAPHY
MACHINE KNITTING NEWS
KNITTING • GUILD OF MASTER
CRAFTSMEN NEWS

The above represents a full list of all titles currently
published or scheduled to be published.
All are available direct from the Publishers or
through bookshops and specialist retailers. To place an
order, or to obtain a complete catalogue, contact:

**GMC Publications,
Castle Place, 166 High Street, Lewes,
East Sussex BN7 1XU United Kingdom
Tel: 01273 488005 Fax: 01273 402866
E-mail: pubs@thegmcgroup.com
Website: www.gmcbooks.com**

Orders by credit card are accepted